HIRING A SUPERSTAR

THE ULTIMATE TALENT FINDER TOOLKIT
FIND, HIRE & KEEP THE BEST PEOPLE FOR YOUR BUSINESS

ADAM BUTLER

First Edition

Copyright © 2014 Adam Butler
Illustrations by Rebecca Emery
All rights reserved.
ISBN: 978-1497578845

For more about the author, please visit:
http://www.adambutlerltd.co.uk

To Danielle.
None of this could have happened without you. Thanks for putting up with me
every day. Love you always. Sorry about the socks... (PRIVATE JOKE!)

- Ad.

TABLE OF CONTENTS

"EUREKA!! I'VE GOT IT!..........oh, um...where is it..........."

INTRODUCTION: MY 'EUREKA' MOMENT

"You cannot change your destination overnight but you can change your direction overnight."

- Jim Rohn

I've been a recruiter in business for over fifteen years now and during that time I've learnt all about what it means to hire the best people. I understand the good, the bad and the ugly of recruitment. I learnt the hard way about discovering the talent that sustains your business long after you've run out of ideas.

I've studied books by Jim Rohn, Stephen Covey and other

esteemed gurus to help me understand what it takes to succeed.

After years of endeavour as a sales rep for several financial service businesses, I finally made it to the 'pinnacle' of what I believed my career could have been at that time. I became the National Sales Manager for a large UK-based motor finance company. Determined to succeed in my new role I was given personal responsibility for the hiring of new staff, either through direct sourcing methods or via recruitment agencies.

It was at this time that I had my 'eureka' moment.

Continually frustrated by the 'chuck enough muck at the wall and some will stick' attitude I encountered, usually within the larger recruitment agencies, and facing a watershed moment in my own career, the penny finally dropped with a resounding clang.

I figured that with my skills, personality and tenacity (motor dealers can present a challenge to even the most patient individual) a career in recruitment could offer a quicker path to my personal success, from both a personal and financial perspective. I'd certainly stumbled upon a yawning gap in the market when it came to customer service and attention to detail.

In 2006 I finally wrote my business plan, and with my parachute prepared and lunch box packed I took the 'entrepreneurs' leap of faith' and made the transition from employed to self-employed. On 26th October 2006 I established the 'imaginatively' named Adam Butler Limited, trading as Adam Butler Associates – a recruitment company that provided search expertise to the motor industry and financial services sectors that I had become so familiar with in the years that preceded.

The first year went great! 2007 saw me achieve all the goals that I had set for my fledgling business, and I worked harder and faster than ever before, connecting my network of contacts with the ambitious businesses that I was out there talking to. With an average 'placement fee' of £6,000, the money was rolling in, and by the end of that year I was ready to implement my ambitious plans for growth.

I took offices near Chester, employed staff (who promised me the earth!), spent money on equipment, and generally went about increasing my overheads with the reckless abandon of a man who believed he could not fail.

And then the bubble burst.

I was sitting at my desk eating a BLT, sipping on a can of diet coke (I remember it in incredible detail!), when I heard on the radio that Lloyds Bank had taken over HBOS. These were two of my biggest clients at the time and I'd worked bloody hard to win a place on their Preferred Supplier Lists (or PSLs). They represented about 40% of the total fees my business invoiced every month at that point.

Within a couple of months, the rest of my client base had either gone out of business, or merged with a competitor, meaning that clients' priorities had moved from hiring to focusing on making extensive redundancies.

The years from 2008 to 2012 were not great if you were focused only on helping motor dealers, or the financial institutions that supported them, to find staff. It was rare that anyone was hiring, and when they occasionally did, no one was prepared to pay fees.

With the 'Credit Crunch' now very evident, I realised I needed to apply the philosophies of Charles Darwin in order to survive. To paraphrase:

"It is not the strongest of the species that survives, nor the most intelligent. It is the one most adaptable to change."

I figured that to survive I would need to adapt. I figured that companies of all types in every location and industry would still need staff and I also concluded that in tough economic conditions they would still want the best, but would not be as willing to pay large agency fees in order to find them.

I realised that I had become an expert in 'sourcing techniques'. I knew how to write exceptional advertising copy that would attract the best, I knew how to head hunt from any pool on behalf of clients in one sector, and I knew that I could adapt those skills to any other industry.

I also knew that I had an excellent understanding of the most up-to-date social media, job-board advertising and CV-searching techniques.

So in 2009 I launched EasyOnlineRecruitment.co.uk – an innovative brokered advertising, resource and response-management solution that provided our clients with the best talent available.

I knew I needed to build my own team around me, starting from scratch, and so once again I packed the lunch box and my parachute, ready to begin again.

As any entrepreneur will tell you, creating your own brand and establishing a business is fun and fulfilling but it also presents considerable challenges. Recruiting people for people requires resilience, patience, determination, discernment, commitment and a big dose of humour.

I understand your pain!

One of the cruellest ironies of running a recruitment business is of course that, as with all businesses, it needs the right team in order to succeed. Hand on heart, I have to confess here and now that the biggest learning curve for me was in grasping the fact that the key to success in recruitment is all about matching the person to the culture of the business.

First of all, however, you have to define and understand that culture for yourself!

My first ever employee was a nightmare who failed to reflect my values, my aims, or my personality. When he promised me the earth (or annual billings of £250k at any rate, which every recruiter will know are the words you long to hear) I took him at his word.

Sadly, he failed to deliver.

I am a great believer in learning from your mistakes and, on reflection, my gut instinct told me he wasn't the right candidate for the job from day one, but...

Eighteen months later he eventually left, taking with him a big chunk of my turnover and clients with him. While he had been 'working' for me, he was also quietly establishing his own recruitment agency.

To quote writer and lecturer Dale Carnegie, *"The successful man will profit from his mistakes and try again in a different way."*

My philosophy these days is to first assess a potential hire's attitude, personality and aspirations in terms of how they match up to my own goals and personality. Through experience I have learnt that candidates frequently perform better at interviews than they do in an actual role, so I've adopted a different approach to my interview techniques.

Today I encourage what I like to call the 'throw out the desk' mentality, asking candidates to carry out during the hiring process a series of group exercises relevant to the job function. This enables me to observe them over a longer period of time and more accurately assess both their ability and personality.

It's a bit like being a successful manager of a football club in the transfer window (I would imagine!) when a manager has his sights set firmly on a particular player. That favoured player may tell you what you want to hear and regale you with glorious stories about the best goals he's ever scored, but that doesn't mean he's perfect for you. How will he fit within your team? Will his natural position suit your overall strategy and goals? How does he interact with your players? Would you allow him to play without undergoing a full medical to check for any underlying problems?

In the same way, assessment tools such as psychometric testing, assessment centres and reference checks are useful in the pursuit of recruiting your superstar, but they are only parts of the jigsaw puzzle that give you a clue to the overall picture, rather than the picture in its entirety.

Ultimately, understanding the culture of your business, together with its needs, values and your personality, is most important – together with TRUSTING YOUR GUT INSTINCT!

Your gut instinct will give you a great intuition for the candidate as a person, as well as whether their attitude matches not only your own but also the 'fabric' of your organisation. Don't fall into the trap of just hiring people like you (is there anyone?), as many entrepreneurs often go looking for a 'mini me' and often that doesn't exist. If you've started a business from scratch then it's your baby, and no one else will ever love it or care about it as much as you.

Recognising this is crucial, so be prepared to build a team of people that share the same beliefs, but who specialise in things that complement your own skill set. The strength of a team lies in its shared beliefs and in its differences. I really believe that.

My biggest lesson when I started EasyOnlineRecruitment.co.uk was centred in the deep understanding of what a business is – what it really does - and what it stands for, that makes the difference. Not just WHAT it does, but more importantly WHY it does it. Getting 'on the bus' people that share these beliefs is crucial, and whilst modern or traditional search techniques are very important, starting with the end in mind is the real key.

We'll look through all these things in what follows, but that's enough about me for now. I am sure that what you are actually waiting for is the secret of how to hire the superstars that will propel your business forward. Well, I have great news for you – that is EXACTLY what this book is about.

After a brief history of the evolution of the recruitment industry, I will take you through the following ESSENTIAL ELEMENTS every brand needs to be successful in its quest to not only attract but RETAIN SUPERSTARS, covering:

Culture Shock – The importance of aligning your core values and culture with your hiring strategy in order to understand precisely the type of talent your organisation needs.

The Hiring Process – Incorporating the 3Ms into a detailed breakdown of each vital stage of your recruitment strategy, including the top six 'must-haves' for every job advert, the top three interview tips for successful interviews, the five signs of a toxic organisation, how to deal with the counter offer and five ways to enhance your job offer (and much more besides).

Always Looking – Why your search for talent should be a long-term strategy, not a response to an immediate requirement.

Playing For Keeps – It's about retaining as well as recruiting. In this section you will find eight essential ingredients for employee retention.

You will also find a review on the cost of a bad hire, as well as tips on how to integrate Millennials into your company and some useful examples of competency- and non-competency based questions to assist with your next round of interviews.

Let's be honest. As I said before, no one will ever care about your business like you do, but if you are serious about achieving 'super success', you will inevitably need help. To that end, you need to find the right people for the right reasons at the right price.

You need to find the superstars. Let's find out how.

"LOOK! OUR PERFECT CANDIDATE, 18 mutual friends, likes Lionel Richie and loves bacon! Thank you Facebook!"

SECTION ONE: THE EVOLUTION OF THE RECRUITMENT INDUSTRY

Before we take the first steps, it's useful to take a look back to see how far recruitment has come in recent years.

Recruitment has evolved considerably in the last twenty years, even gaining a new name in the process (talent acquisition).

Gone are the days when executive recruiters painstakingly and copiously copied out their notes onto candidate and client cards, which served as a 'database'.

Promoting your vacancies back then generally consisted of placing an advert in a relevant media outlet, such as a local newspaper, trade magazine or, for senior roles, the Sunday broadsheets. Applications would roll in, received in hard copy form with handwritten cover letters. To supplement their hiring efforts, 'personnel' managers, as they were often called 'back in the day', may have examined their 'Rolodex' collection of business cards or 'phoned a friend' to see if they 'knew anyone' suitable for a particular role.

Recruitment agencies were frequently employed, but the system used was essentially the same. The most exotic method of forwarding a set of shortlisted CVs was via the fax machine. Interviews were arranged by telephone or letter and the whole process was relatively straightforward. Shortlisted candidates attended an interview and were informed of the decision to hire within anything from a few days to weeks later. This may have been by telephone, but more often than not it would be by letter.

Let's skip forward and see how the world of recruitment has changed.

At one stage, there was talk of the Internet bringing about the demise of recruitment agencies and the need for extensive HR departments. Recruitment agencies, it was believed, would become defunct, with specialist job websites eliminating any need for employers to ever consult an agency again.

Companies would simply place their vacancies on websites and candidates would come to them. The only dilemma they envisaged was the dilemma of choice. We now know that this notion is far from the truth. Celebrating the recruitment industry's gradual slide into extinction was a hasty and somewhat premature conception.

Recruitment and HR specialists have responded to the challenge and grabbed change as an opportunity with both hands. While networking has always been a key part of the recruitment professional's role, the type of networking has changed beyond all comparison. Social networking is simply one more tool in the recruiter's box and it has become one of the most effective. Sites like *Facebook*, *Twitter* and *LinkedIn* have only served to strengthen the recruiter's position.

For recruitment professionals, *LinkedIn* in particular has brought about significant breakthroughs in the way that candidates are suitably located and identified. *LinkedIn* is a dream tool for reviewing the backgrounds of applicants for roles and also unearthing that elusive candidate for that vital company role. In many ways, *LinkedIn* is the 'Rolodex 2.0' of yesteryear, as when a contact moves company they usually always update their *LinkedIn* profile. As a result, you'll always be in touch. Previously, you would have been left with a useless business card containing irrelevant out-of-date details, but with *LinkedIn*, the 'candidate' will do the hard work of updating your database for you.

In addition, the international reach of job boards such as *Monster*, *CareerBuilder*, *Totaljobs* and aggregator sites like *indeed* have all but rendered newspaper adverts obsolete.

They are out of date as soon as the 'sits vac' column goes to press, and by tomorrow they are only really good for wrapping up fish and chips! With job boards and the latest apps, vacancy lists are constantly updated. Job applications made by mobile devices are soaring and applicant-tracking systems (ATS) are habitually used to screen out candidates whose keywords don't make the grade.

We'll be considering the impact of social media in hiring a superstar in more detail in Section Four.

For now, let's bring ourselves to the starting point of the recruitment process.

"That's our new Mission statement. We wrote it the same day we
we switched to decaf."

Section Two: Culture Shock

"Your brand is your culture."

- Tony Hsieh

Talent acquisition is changing more rapidly than any other part of
recruitment, via social recruiting, networking, Big Data and the
variety of recruiting platforms available. Companies will need to
tap into these changes to retain relevance in their employee
brand.

One of the major barriers to achieving business goals in recent
years has been the shortage of available talent, especially in the

global downturn.

As economies around the world now emerge from the longest and most challenging recession in living memory, the market is becoming increasingly candidate-centric. You may not want to hear this, but the power is firmly in the hands of the superstars you seek. It doesn't mean that your hiring strategy is out of your control, only that in order to stay ahead of the competition it is likely that you will have to review your whole recruitment strategy and hiring process as it stands.

This may sound like a radical step but that's what this book is all about – and if it means you find the superstars that help you achieve your goals, then believe me, it's worth it.

Consultant firm Deloitte's latest Human Capital Trends report, issued at the end of 2013, identified *'retention, engagement and attraction of talent'* as the primary challenges facing global employers. In fact, Deloitte has gone so far as to suggest that the 'war' in competing for talent has become the 'war to develop talent'.

The prerequisite to developing talent is attracting the talent (or superstars) in the first place. Engagement and retention strategies then become the top priorities, but all of these processes begin with the culture of your organisation.

To build what employers sometimes refer to as a 'talent community' or talent pool takes a great deal of time, effort, investment, consistency and a clearly defined brand.

Today's workplace is evolving and by 2025, the so-called Millennials (Generation Y) will represent 75% of the global workforce – but they aren't just tomorrow's consideration. In the next few years, Millennials will represent around one third of the workforce and with them comes a different set of expectations. Their aspirations will have a direct impact on how the search for superstar talent is conducted and adapted by most companies. In

Appendix Two I've included six tips for integrating Millennials into your workforce.

Millennials are looking for meaning in their work but they are not alone in this pursuit. It is no longer just about who can offer the best salaries, which is great news for SMEs. A competitive salary is essential of course, but surveys carried out by companies such as *CareerBuilder* have consistently revealed that the priorities in accepting a job offer include:

Work/life balance – Flexible working hours are consistently highlighted as a key attraction and relate highly to the probability of a candidate accepting a job offer.

Company culture – Shrewd talent looks for a positive experience of your company's culture, which begins before you invite them for interview. We'll be considering how to identify and understand your company culture shortly in this chapter.

Employee recognition – Acknowledge your employees through bonuses, plain and simple 'thank yous' and the intangibles that make a difference to their lives, such as sponsored training, book tokens, employee of the month awards, or whatever else it is that makes them feel like a valued part of your company. A company that values its employees generally enjoys higher levels of retention. This is something I endeavour to instil in all my clients time and again.

Leadership – Actions speak louder than words. A clearly communicated vision and an approachable boss who is willing to listen – this represents only the tip of the iceberg when it comes to defining good leadership.

Continuous career development – Talented performers are always looking for ways they can improve their skills and build on their experience. A company that offers its employees on-going mentoring and career development opportunities will not only attract but retain those ambitious superstars.

This doesn't preclude salary of course, but it is not necessarily the over-riding influence in the accepting of a position. There has to be more to a career move than an improvement on salary but still, it MUST be a competitive salary. That is a given throughout this process.

It begins with you, your brand, making your whole candidate experience consistently appealing to the superstars your business needs. To understand this, however, you need to understand your company's culture and what it is you want to achieve.

ALIGNING CULTURE WITH VALUES AND BUILDING POSITIVE LEADERSHIP

Aligning your culture with your values is essential in your quest to hire the superstars you seek. It's something that I discuss and evaluate with each of my clients on a regular basis before launching a search.

As an employer, whether you are on your first hire or your one thousandth, the principles for successful recruitment remain the same.

It is essential to match the culture and values of your organisation with the talent you bring in.

More often than not, I am presented with a long list of essential skills, qualifications and achievements by the employers looking to fill a key vacancy within their company.

What they rarely tell me about, without a bit of cajoling and in-depth questioning, is what the culture of their company is like and, equally as important, what success looks like in their business. What key traits do their most successful people have? What would they like more of? What would they like less of?

Aligning your culture with your core values is the biggest single thing you can do to influence, attract and retain your superstars. Let me say that again because it bears repeating and, if you get this part right, the rest should fall slowly but surely into place.

Aligning your culture with your core values is the biggest single thing you can do to influence, attract and retain your superstars.

Look at your culture like it is the 'personality' of your business, developing over time. As a child, it needs nurturing and encouragement to develop positive personality traits and discourage negative attributes. In the beginning, this requires hard work, dedication and commitment. Over time, a child learns to stand on its own two feet and matures into the person you want it to be.

Your business is the same, but occasionally there is some discipline required, or a slight adjustment of culture to get it back on track.

Two great books I have read on the subject of culture are *'Delivering Happiness'* by Tony Hsieh and *'Start With Why'* by Simon Sinek, which have become two of my recruitment 'bibles' over my many years in business. Not because they are specifically about RECRUITMENT – they aren't! More because they talk in such detail about understanding 'WHY' companies do what they do, what they care about, and what they believe in. When this is outlined and understood, it's much more straightforward to go about finding a 'crew' to help you row your boat.

Here we'll look at ways in which you can develop your own company culture.

The McKinsey organisation once referred to culture as *"how we do things around here."* That's culture in a nutshell, but it doesn't necessarily mean it is the right way to do things or that it corresponds with your core values.

Culture is never as important as when it's no longer working or attracting the superstars you need into your business.

Problems with culture often rise sharply into focus when organisations go through change, when companies merge and two disparate cultures come together, or when a company's success requires it to evolve and change its culture to accommodate its need for more defined strategies. In these cases, staying with the culture you began with can hinder your growth, rather than support it.

Typical signs of a bad culture include the following:

- High levels of employee turnover or absenteeism

- Low morale (carry out an employee survey if you dare!)

- Lack of candidates responding to your job adverts

- Candidates falling out of your pipeline before completing the interview process

- High levels of candidate turndowns of your job offers.

To ensure that the culture of your company matches up to its core values, it is essential to examine and assess the level of co-ordination between them. You need to scrutinise whether or not your culture accurately reflects your core values and, if it doesn't, to identify the differences.

This is where you will need to make the changes to ensure you can attract the superstars you need.

A client of ours – one of the fastest growing businesses in the Midlands if not the UK – tests culture match from potential employees from the very first interaction it has with them. Not only does it talk about its 'Why' in the recruitment advertising and agency briefings, as well as directing applicants to a web-based landing page with a video explaining "what it's like round here", it also does something unusual at the interview stage.

You see, our client believes in working hard, going the extra mile, and delivering on promises to clients as well as one another within the organisation. So the initial 'interview' is a group meeting, where the simple instruction is to arrive at the company's offices at 5.36pm. It is explained to the candidates that they can arrive six minutes early (no more than that as nobody likes someone waiting in reception for 30 minutes!), but they cannot arrive one minute late. People who do not follow that instruction to the letter do not get into the 'process'.

The client tells me that as a result of this initial screening process, coupled of course with some additional tests and investigation, the retention rate of staff has gone through the roof, and the productivity of his team has doubled over the last 12 months since its introduction. It can only be because the expectation has been set early, and the number-one priority is to achieve a match of culture from the outset.

How could you adapt something similar in your initial screening process?

UNDERSTANDING YOUR CORE VALUES

This book is about hiring superstars, rather than determining your company's core values, but some time spent in doing just that will help you to find and hire those superstars.

In my experience, it's essential to understand that core values are not strategies. Core values are fixed – strategies change and adapt all the time.

As a guideline, I've listed ten common core values that I see on a daily basis while working with a range of clients, from fledgling

SMEs to corporate organisations:

- Commitment

- Work/life balance

- Accountability

- Diversity

- Community

- Empowerment

- Innovation

- Integrity

- Health & safety

- Ownership.

What you cover within those core values is down to you as a company and organisation.

UNDERSTANDING YOUR CULTURE TODAY

To help you to evaluate your culture, you will need to ask the following questions of your company:

- What do your employees think of you? (Have you carried out an employee survey? If you haven't I recommend you do so at your earliest opportunity).

- What reputation do you have with your clients, target audience and your shareholders?

- What do recent press releases say about your company (if relevant)?

- What is being said about your company on *Glassdoor*? (For those of you who have not encountered *Glassdoor*, I'll explain what it is shortly).

- What do these stories say about what your organisation believes in?

- What is your unique selling point?

- Do you carry out customer service reviews?

- What do your employees expect of you?

- How do you deal with problems within your organisation?

- What core values does your response suggest?

- Is your organisation a flat or hierarchical structure, formal or informal?

- Do you promote from within or always bring in new staff for a key role?

- Are your controls stringent?

- Do you reward your teams for commitment over and above the call of duty?

- How do you measure quality of service?

- What does your leadership say about you?

Answers to these and similar questions will enable you to build a strong picture of your culture and identify your brand values.

Once you have these answers, you can understand how your culture matches up to your values – or not.

If you have identified a gap between your culture and your core values, this may be hindering your ability to attract the superstars that will benefit your business.

Before you recruit one more person into your business it is also VITALLY IMPORTANT to understand what is causing this gap, so you can take steps to rectify the problem.

The following questions will help:

- What strengths and weaknesses can you identify in your culture?

- What is preventing you from establishing a culture that reflects your core values?

- What factors are negatively impacting the health, safety, wellbeing and productivity of your teams?

- Which elements of your culture will you retain and which will you change?

- What types of positive behaviour and beliefs do you need to encourage?

- Does your social media presence reflect your core values?

Social media plays a key part in the promotion of your brand, which we will consider in Section Four of this book.

SIX QUICK TIPS FOR IMPROVING YOUR CULTURE

As a quick summary before we begin to examine the hiring process itself, you may want to think about the following.

While these tips are 'quick' to deliver, they are not necessarily easy to implement, and each one could form a whole chapter of their own:

Articulate your brand message: Once you thoroughly understand your core values, these should be incorporated within your company's vision and inform everything you do. *Clue: it begins at the top.* Poor leadership permeates through your whole company.

Listen! Don't shrink back from carrying out an employee survey. Be open to employee suggestions and don't be afraid to admit your mistakes. Errors are always a learning opportunity and believe me, I've made a few!

Your workforce is evolving, so should you: The most successful companies evolve with their workforce and manage a smooth integration of new arrivals with more established performers. Implementing a mentoring strategy can offer benefits to everyone involved.

Allow your talent room to manoeuvre: Allow your superstars – and your company – to grow through performance reviews, training schemes and mentoring to nurture your talent and encourage them to develop and improve.

Identify the gap between your core values and your culture: And be bold enough to take steps to close it. Enough said! (Employee survey anyone?)

Examine your leadership team: A positive company culture that attracts, retains and develops the superstars it needs relies on credible and ethical leadership. What does your leadership team (which may be just *you* in a small business!) say about the culture of your company?

Getting your attitude right is the single most important thing you can do to ensure your culture and values are represented by the people working in your business on a day-to-day basis.

Don't get me wrong – aptitude is also key, but you should always look at attitude first.

It is much easier to train, coach and develop candidates with potential and give them the technical skills they may lack. It is so much harder to change the inherent character traits of a person, and even harder to get rid of a bad attitude!

Tony Hsieh talks about this extensively in his book *'Delivering Happiness'*. One technique that really demonstrates the Zappos (that's his company) commitment to attaining this culture match is what I call their $2,000 leap of faith.

You see, when a new colleague joins Zappos they undergo an intensive four-week training programme, immersing them in the company's strategy, culture and processes. About one week into this, Zappos makes what it calls 'The Offer', where it tells these new starters: "If you leave today we will pay you for the work you have done, plus we will give you a one-time $2,000 bonus to leave us."

The amazing thing is that because people have really bought in to the culture by then, only a tiny percentage of people take the offer (less than 2% at the time of writing).

To me this is an outstanding (and brave!) statement of confidence that Zappos has in its recruiting and induction procedure. Hsieh speaks extensively about always making a culture match first, before finding out about a skill match. The belief it has in this process is demonstrated in the $2,000 offer to every employee that comes up the ranks.

Sure, some people take the cash, but the truth is they would be the ones that would perhaps have left anyway after a short period of time.

It's a bold move, but how could you adapt something similar into your business?

Within my own business, we have a set of 'golden rules' that we incorporate from the very first contact we have with potential candidates, whether this is through adverts, initial conversations, induction, or even regular appraisal. By clearly laying out these expectations both at an early stage and throughout the employee's career with us, we find there are fewer surprises later on in the cycle, thus enhancing the likelihood of a great candidate match. A good candidate is one that arrives, stays and performs at a high and consistent level.

On top of that, it saves us time and improves our recruitment techniques if we continually fine-tune our systems and methodology.

If you ever visit our offices you will see our GOLDEN RULES proudly and prominently displayed in reception and elsewhere in the business. I've put them on the wall behind the sink, but stopped short of putting them up in the toilets!

They are what I believe, and what my management team believes. The golden rules are our expectations, and anyone that doesn't think they are right or fair can hop off the bus any time. Interestingly, though, since we started weaving the golden rules into the fabric of the business, not many people have left. I think it's because everyone knows where they stand from the get go.

Here are our Golden Rules. Please feel free to adapt these for your own business:

Adam Butler Limited/EasyOnlineRecruitment.co.uk

"GOLDEN RULES"

We want everyone that works with us to be *inspired!* We want you to enjoy working as part of a friendly and highly successful team, working hard and respecting one another. We want you to be rewarded for the good work you do. Above all, we want you to enjoy working here, and these standards help us all to know what is expected of one another.

---

1. We work a Fair and Full day

This means that time at work is spent productively! Personal stuff needs to be kept to a minimum. This includes taking personal calls, sending texts, checking personal social media channels (**unless it's to find and connect with GREAT TALENT for one of our awesome clients!**)

2. We are a Team

We're all in this together. Being a team means that saying or thinking "It's not my job" is unacceptable.

3. We're Proud of Our Work

Because we take pride in our work, we do it as it is intended to be done. No shortcuts, omissions, bodge-jobs or work-arounds! We will support every employee who does deliver a fair, just, full day of compliant work, by not saddling them with the slack of any bad employees.

4. We Respect Our Customers & Candidates

Our **customers and candidates are the reason we come to work every day** – and we remember this when we speak to them by phone, email or face to face. They pay our wages and are the reason for our existence. We always seek to understand them, to see things from their point of view and deliver WORLD CLASS SERVICE to them at all times.

5. We Keep Our Promises

When we say we'll do something or we'll get back to someone, we do it. We don't let people down – colleagues, customers or suppliers.

6. We're Positive

It's NEVER OK to say negative things about the company or any of our customers, staff or suppliers. We won't tolerate – at all – anything or anyone that contributes negative word of mouth.

7. We Do Things Quickly

We don't do things slowly. We do them quickly or not at all. This means that there'll always be lots going on – and things will change as we adapt and spot new opportunities. It's never been calm around here, and as long as we're successful, it never will be!

8. We're In Business To Make Profit

We're not here just for fun (although fun is hopefully a great bonus of enjoying your work here and the people in your team!) Getting and keeping profitable customers is the most important thing we do. Creating profit is fundamental to any successful company and the people we value most are the ones who contribute most to profit. It's not enough to be busy. As teams and as individuals, we need to ask ourselves "What are we busy doing?" If you're not focusing on profit, you're doing something wrong... It's OK for anybody to question anybody else, at any time about what they're doing and how it contributes to profit.

9. We Finish Stuff

Our key measures of success and performance will be based around what you got done, not what you are doing. We don't like activity masquerading as accomplishment – you need to focus on getting things done. Not 'doing' or 'in the pipeline', but properly done. Finished. Crossed Off. Achieved.

10. We Recognise and Reward Good Thinking

We can all find better, more efficient ways to do stuff – and we've all got a responsibility to speak up and share those thoughts.

11. We Think Before We Act

Making an honest mistake when you've thought something through and did things for the right reasons is fine. In fact it's encouraged. However, doing something dumb because you didn't think it through or care enough is unacceptable.

12. We Don't Clock-Watch

Working at Adam Butler Limited/EasyOnlineRecruitment means putting in some extra hours. This isn't 'face-time' - we do it because we enjoy working here and we believe in what we're doing and want to get the job done quickly and as effectively as possible!

13. We Work Hard, Play Hard and Eat Lunch

We make time every day for breaks and to refresh ourselves. We all need breaks to work effectively.

14. We Keep Our Workplace Tidy

Everything should have a home – we don't let stuff congregate by the sides of desks, in corridors, in reception, or under the stairs.

"First, as an ice breaker... how many of you have tattoos?"

SECTION THREE: THE HIRING PROCESS

"The secret of my success is that we have gone to exceptional lengths to hire the best people in the world."

- Steve Jobs

THE '3 MS'

From my time in recruitment, if there is one thing I have observed, it is the importance of marketing.

Most companies today forget, or perhaps have yet to learn, that recruitment/talent acquisition, whatever you prefer to call it, is in fact a MARKETING conundrum. It is the act of making you or your organisation so irresistible to others that they are intrigued to discover more!

In all of your marketing strategies, understanding the 3 M's and getting them in the correct order is fundamental to your success.

MARKETING – WHO are you targeting? You need to be SUPER clear on this before you proceed to the next stage. What will your superstar look like? Where do they live? What are their hobbies and interests? What are their inspirations? What do they read? Consider creating an AVATAR of this person. Give them a name, understand who they are, so that when they walk into your office you will recognise them instantly (I'm referring to their attributes rather than a literal recognition).

MESSAGE – Once you have identified the 'who', you can craft your MESSAGE. What will motivate them? Will it be money, benefits, career, training, development, responsibility or ego?

How will you attract them? For SMEs who consider themselves to be at a disadvantage, remember, big doesn't necessarily mean better. Smaller companies can offer more flexibility and more opportunities for superstars to broaden their experience. Larger organisations will often have more defined HR strategies that restrict their ability to be flexible, but if you are a larger business reading this then perhaps adopting greater flexibility means that you can stay ahead of your competition and get the very best people in.

MEDIA – Once you understand your vision of who it is you want to attract, you need to begin to engage with these people. Engagement with talented performers starts long before the hiring process. Use media, whether it's social media, the national press, trade press, job boards or recruitment agencies (which are essentially just another, admittedly higher investment, media channel). Superstars need a reason to pursue opportunities with your company before your job vacancy appears.

BEGIN WITH THE JOB DESCRIPTION

A brief note on the 'knee-jerk' hire

Before we move on, I have one note of caution which comes directly from painful personal experience. What I mean by a 'knee-jerk' hire is the occasions when a long-term or established team member suddenly leaves you. It's natural in your instant panic at their 'betrayal' to replace 'like for like'.

My advice is DON'T!

Sometimes it's not always the right thing to do.

Every time someone leaves your company it provides you with a great opportunity to analyse and consider the balance and ability of your remaining team and identify where the skills gap within your business lies.

Review your organisation as a whole and consider the possibility of up-skilling a member of your existing team to bridge the gap left by your erstwhile team member.

It won't work in every case but it is always worth pausing for breath!

Some time ago, I lost two senior members of my sales team at the same time. It's a long story. In a nutshell, they tried to set up in competition against me.

While hiring two identical replacements was my original (knee-jerk) reaction, I did in fact pause for breath and took stock of the situation to evaluate what I needed before setting out on my next hire. As it turns out, it was easier to increase the levels of administrative support within the business rather than recruit two more sales people. By working more efficiently, productivity – and subsequently sales – soared.

I'm not saying you don't need to replace 'like for like', but I am recommending that you consider all of the options before diving in.

Anyway, I digress. Let's get back to your hiring strategy and job description.

Once you understand the culture of your company, this will help you to realign your hiring strategy with the type of talent you need to achieve your goals. From here, it all starts with the job description.

Before we go any further, there's one piece of advice that I've found invaluable for larger companies with HR departments and it's this – **it is essential to get HR buy-in to your job description.** This will prevent problems during the candidate-screening period. It will also enable you to focus on what you are really looking for from your successful candidate, which isn't only the job description, but your performance management criteria – i.e. what do you want the successful candidate to achieve in this role?

This is a crucial part of the process, as the type of talent you attract will depend on the effectiveness of your job advert, which is derived from your job description.

Talent management – or finding the superstars – requires an evolution in traditional procedures. If this is an existing position, please resist the urge to dig out the original job description, dust it off and put your standard advert out there (knee jerk!)

Now is your opportunity to do things differently!

"If you always do what you've always done, you'll always get what you've always gotten."

- Tony Robbins

Of course, if you're happy and confident that what you are doing is attracting exactly the talent you need within your organisation, then that's great.

In that case, my advice should reaffirm your existing strategy.

As a guideline, every job description should incorporate the following key points:

The job itself: What tasks will the candidate actually complete in the job on a daily basis? What does a typical working week consist of? Who will the successful candidate be interacting with in this role? What will the title of the position be and is this consistent with similar positions in your industry? If you give a job the title of 'Coordinator' and other companies use the term 'Executive', your advert is probably going to be ignored in favour of something more exciting (we'll look at job titles when posting your job ad online a little later).

Summarise up to half a dozen key responsibilities in the position but be sure to be specific. If you're not certain, how can you attract the ideal candidate you need, or even hope to define who they are?

Experience: Exactly what experience is ESSENTIAL? I emphasised 'essential' because I've sometimes worked with organisations who have given me a list of 'essential' criteria that has effectively ruled out some great talent. There's a significant difference between 'must-have' and 'nice to have'.

Are you 100% certain each criteria is a 'must-have?' Consider what is essential in areas such as practical knowledge, qualifications, industry experience and achievements – but don't rule out 'close match' candidates who possess transferable skills. These are candidates with the potential, the right attitude and ability to become tomorrow's superstars.

Naturally, there will be a set of 'minimum criteria' for each position, but in keeping the parameters for this 'minimum criteria' too narrow, you may deter a future superstar from giving your advert more than a cursory glance.

It's my firmly held belief that ATTITUDE is king in the world of talent. Get someone with the right attitude that matches your expectations. Someone that has potential, but not necessarily experience. Give them the right support and watch them fly! Experience can be gained, but attitude can rarely be changed, so don't be wooed by the ten years of corporate experience, or five years of software coding, unless the attitude is a match!

Candidate skills: What are the unique skills that will separate the high achiever from the run-of-the-mill candidate? Defining what performance criteria must be met in this role will enable you to agree on the skills required. List the technical skills but don't forget the soft skills too. Again, it comes back to potential. A candidate with a positive outlook and the ability to learn quickly can acquire the technical skills needed for a role.

Once again, take it from me – you can't buy attitude.

This was brought home to me when I took on two apprentices in my business at exactly the same time for exactly the same position – that of a Resourcer. Essentially, I needed a recruitment administrator to free up my consultants' time for speaking to candidates and clients.

There wasn't a huge number of applications for the position of apprentice, and I was looking for virtually no unique skills – just a bright and positive attitude with decent ability for web searching and using Microsoft Office.

At the assessment centre that we ran, these two candidates really stood out from the crowd, both demonstrating a bright and friendly personality, and showing signs of ambition to learn and develop quickly. Long story short, I offered them both a job.

Very quickly after starting with us one of the apprentices, Tahlia Roberts, really started to shine, grasping the opportunity and demonstrating potential far in excess of what we would have hoped for. The other apprentice was the polar opposite – lacking energy and the ability to think on her own initiative. Her PC and Internet skills were way below what we had originally thought, and her all-round attitude was poor, with her always showing up late and leaving dead on time.

Tahlia has gone on to be promoted to Account Manager in our business and shows all the signs of making it as a real superstar. The other apprentice has gone. She would have stayed but I took the decision to 'Get rid quickly', as she didn't have the right attitude or align with enough of our golden rules.

At the end of the day, because they were both apprentices and I hired them simultaneously, it did not cost me a lot of actual cash in terms of layout, but their opportunity potential was huge. Because of her outstanding attitude and work ethic, Tahlia saw this and grabbed it.

The story above just goes to underline that it is more about attitude than just skills, as skills can be developed quickly. It also shows that you can only hope to get it right more often than you get it wrong. And when you do get it wrong, you will know it in your gut. My advice here is hire slowly and fire quickly. At the end of the day, you will know what is the best thing to do for your business.

Some of you may be thinking, "How come even Adam gets it wrong?" Well, the truth is that as an entrepreneur you have to take risks, and two apprentices represent a really low risk to me and my business, but the potential return on investment is huge, as demonstrated with Tahlia working out so well. If I had been recruiting a new Sales Director or Finance Director, the risk would have been much greater, and getting it wrong could have been much more damaging with far-reaching implications for my business. In that case, I would take much more time in the hiring process and be less willing to just 'give someone a chance'.

Business, at the end of the day, is about knowing what you want and being prepared to take some calculated risks along the way in order to achieve your goals. If you risk nothing, you may well end up risking everything.

Personality and Style of Working: In small businesses, this becomes especially important as the wrong hire disrupts a team and impacts on the day-to-day running of the business. How will the successful candidate get the job done? Will they need to work closely with others or is the role autonomous? What characteristics do your most successful employees share? Take a look back at your core values and your business culture and write down the personal attributes you value the most highly. These may include compassion, integrity and a sense of humour. They aren't necessarily traits to list in a job advert, but they will help during the screening and initial interview process.

From here you can begin to develop the profile of who you want to appeal to. They are your "Market" and remember it is **Market that you need to consider first before thinking about the Message OR Media!**

ENSURE YOUR JOB ADVERT GETS READ

Once you've assessed the culture of your business and you understand what it is that you are looking for in your next hire, it's time to prepare your job advert.

I have another important question for you before we continue.

Where is the BUZZ in this job?

A generic or mediocre job description won't attract the superstars you need to fulfil your goals and achieve your vision. It won't lure the top talent away from their current employer.

You need colour – you need excitement! Without that your job advert won't stand out from the crowd. And if you don't stand out from the crowd, how can you attract the superstars that do?

This step represents the second of the 3 M's – the **MESSAGE**.

Six Tried And Tested Steps to Creating Your Best Job Advert EVER!

When placing a job advert, you need to consider a number of points:

- Your AVATAR – the type of person you want to attract

- Your core values and culture

- What people want to read!

Sometimes, it's difficult to step back and get perspective on what people will be attracted to. You may think your company offers the ultimate potential, best salaries and the most sizzling opportunities on the market – and it may well be true.

Unless you consider those three elements I outlined above, however, you have no chance of attracting the elusive talent that is out there. *Believe me, it does exist, but it isn't flocking to any old job advert.*

Here are my six tried and tested simple steps to creating your best job advert EVER and attracting the attention of the superstars you need!

Step One: Think hard about your job title – or a combination of Job Titles!

Also, think about the job title in relation to the MEDIA that you are using to attract the person. If you are using newspapers then it's more about the section of the newspaper that you are listed in than the job title, as job seekers looking for sales jobs will go to the sales section first.

So using a more 'out there' job title like SALES ACE, or SALES SUPREMO is fine, as they will 'get it'.

When giving an instruction to a recruitment agency, however, the job title would be unimportant, as the right agency will know what your industry understands that job to be. There are always exceptions to the rule of course, and an agency may advise towards attracting A Players by appealing to the ego of potentials. If it's a senior role, allow them some discretion to advise you. 'Associate Director' can often receive a better response than 'Sales Manager' or 'Key Account Manager'.

Most people have an ego, and want that reflecting in their job title or business card. If that tactic can help you get the best, then use it.

When a candidate searches for a job online using the various job boards, there are only three principal ways of getting found by candidates. This is due to the search functions of the job-board system. You may have the best advert copy ever seen by humanity, but if these three main criteria are not utilised, the best candidates will not find your advert. Here they are:

1. Job Type

2. Salary

3. Location

When job seekers go to the job boards (and all job boards work in broadly the same way), they first have to enter the 'type' of job they are after. That may be Sales, Marketing, Finance, Technical, Engineering – in fact the list is virtually endless, but you need to think like a job seeker and consider what they will be looking for.

Within the consideration of 'job type', you will have room for a job title, and here you again need to think like your prospective employee. If they search for a job title rather than a job type, you may need to think about multiple job titles you can use or include within your advert. Consider conducting some research as to what people in similar positions at your competitors are called.

For instance, the job seeker you want for your sales job may search for Sales Executive, Sales Manager, Account Manager, Business Development Manager, Business Development Executive, or any derivative of those. Your 'job title' for purposes of advertising on job boards can reflect this and look something like this: *'Sales Executive / Business Development / Sales SUPERSTAR!'*

(Please note that you can of course give the position a different title internally when offering the job. The title on your advert is simply to widen the net as far as possible to ensure you appeal to as many of the right types of people as possible.)

Don't use the same order or layout every time you post an ad – mix it up to grab their attention. Don't be afraid to be creative. How many job adverts do you see that are dull and boring and easily skipped over in favour of something more exciting by ambitious superstars? The title is the first thing they will see, so you need to both appeal to your ideal candidate and stand out in a sea of boring jobs. Experiment and see what works for you. If you are going for 'whacky', be sure to include something more mainstream and formal too to show them you are serious.

Catch their attention but make sure that what you are offering backs it up. Don't forget – whatever message you convey to your potential superstars, it must align with your core values and your culture!

A word of warning here:

One client of ours loves to be 'whacky'. At a party its staff would be the 'zany' ones with loud shirts and huge smiles (if you are reading this you know who you are!) – and this is great as it is a key part of their culture.

When writing adverts for them, initially they were insistent that we ONLY used crazy job titles. Things like 'Instant Rapport Creator' or even 'Sorcerer's Apprentice'.

These are perfectly fine – brilliant in fact – for internal job titles, but the problem is that they don't translate into a suitable job title for use online on job boards.

Despite our insistence, they demanded that jobs were listed with their preferred titles only. And guess what happened? Nobody applied – not a soul!

The obvious reason was that no one was out there looking to be hired as an 'Instant Rapport Creator' or 'Sorcerer's Apprentice, or typing those terms into job board search engines. People were much more likely to be looking for jobs as 'Customer Service Advisors' or 'Marketing Graduates'.

Eventually, after a couple of rounds of zero applications, the client took our advice, and we blew them away with the number, and quality, of applicants. It now employs some excellent Instant Rapport Creators and a couple of outstanding Sorcerer's Apprentices that just happened to apply for jobs with much different titles!

Step Two: Use a headline

A job advert is essentially marketing copy, and your headline will make the difference between candidates reading your adverts or moving on to the next vacancy that catches their eye.

Candidates trawl through page after page of job adverts. Your headline must be compelling, sit right at the top of your copy (hence the word *'headline'*...) and be specifically designed to attract your target audience. It's important to be creative but at the same time, if there is one golden rule I've learnt in creating countless job adverts it is this – **AVOID CLICHÉS!**

A cliché is a turnoff.

Typical job-posting clichés include the following (and I'm sure you can think of some more of your own):

- Outstanding growth potential.

- Competitive salary and benefits package.

- Join a fast-paced environment.

- Seeking a highly motivated individual.

What do these words mean? They are generic and typical of the headlines and 'highlights' you will see on many job adverts. More importantly, they will fail to attract the talent your business needs to move ahead and allow you to achieve your goals.

The best headlines are short, snappy one-liners that are guaranteed to stop the superstars in their tracks and encourage them to investigate your opportunity.

I'll share here a great example of what worked well for me recently.

'The best job in the world!'

That's quite a claim to live up to by anyone's standards but it generated a 39.75% increase in candidate responses compared to advertising the same job without a headline.

Step Three: Include salary – and widen your salary banding

How many job adverts do you see that don't include salary?

Given that the majority of people search based on the three main criteria of job type, salary and location, you must not only include salary but also widen your salary banding.

I can hear HR and small business owners swallowing hard at these words, but bear with me on this one and allow me to explain my reasoning. I understand that you want to recruit the very best person for the minimal amount of outlay, but this can be a very real example of 'false economy'.

Let me ask you this:

What would you do if the perfect candidate walked through your door – that elusive superstar with ideal experience and a demonstrable track record of success with your number-one competitor? How would you react if that candidate possessed superlative personal and professional references, was available immediately and even looked and smelled the part of the superstar?

Before you answer, there's one final question.

What would you do if that candidate asked for £1,000 per year more on their basic salary than you had been thinking of advertising this role for?

Would you say 'no'?

I will leave you to ponder on that one.

This is all part of tailoring the Message to suit the Market. The point I'm trying to make here is that you shouldn't think 'bottom end' of your salary range or budget when it comes to your job advert. Forget all of that and ask yourself what is the most you would stretch to for the perfect candidate. Remember, you'll only have to pay it if the perfect candidate does in fact turn up for interview.

What is that figure?

My next suggestion? Widen your salary banding on your job

advert to include your maximum budget. That way your advert will show up in more job searches. Coupled with a great HEADLINE and an equally alluring JOB TITLE, the number of applicants to your vacancy should increase accordingly!

If you're still unconvinced that the investment is worth it, all I can advise you to do is reflect on the information provided on the 'Cost Of A Bad Hire' section in Appendix One of this book – then reconsider your stance on this vital matter. It will take only a few minutes to read but could make the difference between success and stagnation for your business.

Step Four: Keywords

Create your keywords based on the hard and soft skills that emerged during your evaluation of the job description. Job searches are carried out on keywords. Primary keywords include the job title, qualifications and vital skills to guarantee successful performance in the role. Without them, your advert may miss the mark and fail to show up in the job-search results of the superstars you seek.

Keywords are particularly important when using online advertising (job boards), but don't fall into the trap of thinking that keywords are not relevant if you are advertising in the national, local or trade press.

Most of the job boards out there are owned by national or international media groups and, as a result, when you advertise in the press your job will usually find its way online. Ensuring your advert has all the right keywords is therefore critical.

Step Five: Keep it concise

The presentation of your advert matters. Ambitious individuals make quick decisions. They need to swiftly scan and assess what success looks like in this role. Use easily identifiable bullet points, succinct paragraphs, simple fonts and plenty of space between your paragraphs. Too much dense text is a definite 'no-no' and guaranteed to get them moving on.

Think about the CVs you receive. The ones that make easy reading (apart from the content) are concise and succinct with plenty of white space on the page. They tell you everything you need to know in less than 20 seconds (the MAXIMUM time a recruiter gives to a CV).

Just as you will discard a CV that doesn't grab your attention, so will a candidate move on to your competitor's job advert for the same reasons, which brings me to our last point in this section...

Step Six: AIDA

I love AIDA: *Attention, Interest, Desire and Action.*

Without each of these four elements, your advert will fade without trace. Your job title, your headline and your salary will attract attention but, as they say, the devil is in the detail. The job description will inspire superstars to act and apply to your position. Personalise your advert by addressing the candidate directly using 'you' throughout, rather than 'the ideal candidate'.

Attention – This is where your Headline needs to shine

Interest – Here you should focus on getting the job seeker's interest. Rather than just talking about your business, let them see what's in it for them. If you have a market-leading product, or a business that has grown dramatically and outperformed your competition, then here's where to pitch the opportunity.

Desire – You need to develop the candidate's desire to apply. By and large, candidates think as we all do – about themselves first – so consider how they are thinking and write accordingly. Apply the 'WIIFM' factor – 'What's In It For Me?'. If you can show the candidate/job seeker what is in it for them, you are sure to get a great response.

Action – Nothing happens until someone does something, so you need to provide instructions detailing how to apply: email, phone call, written letter or something more creative like a video. Give them multiple options and see who is the most creative.

Note: Getting the candidate to take action is of course critical and in some instances can be a useful selection tool. We have run some campaigns where we asked candidates to prepare a short video of themselves explaining why they were the right person for job. Admittedly, this works with a more extrovert requirement such as sales, but it doesn't always need to be a video. It could be a text, phone call or even fax.

Asking job seekers to do something means that you are limiting your applications to the ones that can read an instruction and be proactive enough to get off their backsides and make stuff happen. Limiting applications can sometimes backfire so perhaps you could put this step in at the next stage of the application process. For instance, do your shortlisting, speak to them, and then ask them to do something for you.

They'll be more inclined to act when they have spoken to you and gained an even better understanding of (and more desire for) the job.

And finally... don't assume you will have candidates tripping over themselves to apply for a position within your company – unless you happen to be a household brand name such as Apple, Microsoft, Google... get the picture? So be prepared to do some selling on the benefits of your business to create that desire.

WHERE HAVE ALL THE CANDIDATES GONE?

All the theory is OK of course, but with one third of employers globally stating that a lack of actual applicants[1] is one of the main reasons they struggle to find sufficient talent to fill key roles, the onus is on you, the employer, to find more ways of reaching your candidates.

If you identify with this issue, first of all you need to re-examine your hiring strategy to ensure your core values and culture align with the image your brand projects.

In the meantime, here are my top five tips that will help you to understand WHY candidates aren't responding to your company adverts.

Glassdoor: If *Glassdoor* to you means the main access to your garden from your house, get ready for a whole new definition! *Glassdoor* is the candidate and employee equivalent of *Tripadvisor*. Employers need to sit up and take notice now. On the pages of *Glassdoor*, employees and candidates post anonymously and share their experiences about what it's really like to work for your company and their experiences in the interview process. *Glassdoor* began life in the US but is slowly gaining a foothold in the UK employment market. Such is its growing influence that in 2013 the CIPD (The Chartered Institute of Personnel and Development) recently sat up and took notice by emphasising its significance to UK employers. My advice is don't see it as a threat – take a leaf out of Unilever's book and regard it as an opportunity. Unilever actively encourages applicants and job seekers to share their experiences with the company on *Glassdoor*. With 75 million page views per month, get ahead of your competition and ensure a great candidate and employee experience and get those reviews onto *Glassdoor*.

Check your mobile presence: How mobile is your careers page? (You have got a careers page right? If not then you need one!) The

---

[1] Source : Manpower

use of mobile devices by candidates is now stratospheric, with 9.3 million workers in March 2013 searching for jobs via a mobile device (that was up from 2.3 million in the previous March). You can only imagine where those figures are at now. Despite this, only a relative handful of companies offer candidates the option of applying for a job via a mobile device. Make it easy for your busy superstars – ensure your application process is mobile friendly. Attract the best talent before your competition! You know it makes sense.

If you're not convinced, consider this fact – 70% of mobile job seekers act within an hour of seeing a vacancy, compared to only 20% of PC users.

What is your Unique Employment Proposition (UEP)? What can you offer your candidates that your closest rivals can't? What keeps your top performers at your company rather than moving to a competitor? If you don't know, it's time to find out. Whatever it is, you need to do more of it. If, on the other hand, your staff turnover is high, there is a flaw in your UEP. Yet again, it's time to find out what it is. Have you carried out an employee satisfaction survey yet? If not, there's no time like the present. Take another look at the questions in the section on culture in Section Two before your recruit your next employee.

Keep your candidates in the pipeline: According to a *CareerBuilder* survey carried out in 2013, a poor experience at interview is one of the main reasons job seekers give for withdrawing their application for a position. I've included a list of the typical signs of a toxic organisation in the next section of this book, which covers the interview itself. If you answer 'yes' to even one statement, you need to overhaul your hiring process.

Make it easy for candidates to apply: Guard against all that time and commitment you put into creating your job advert going to waste. Make it easy for talent to apply either via email, online submissions or even by snail mail if necessary. Sometimes the best candidates will send a hard copy of their CV, knowing that the chances of you seeing it are higher than submitting it to the ATS (Applicant Tracking Systems) 'machines'. Clearly state your application deadline so all candidates have an idea of when to expect a response.

Remember what I said about requesting an unusual application, for instance via video or text? Well, you also need to remember that the talent that is actively job-searching will be bombarded by other vacancies, which could be much easier to apply for than yours. The real key is for you to build the desire (the 'D' in AIDA), and motivate the talent to really need to reach out to you and impress.

Put some of the 'human' back into your HR strategy: As a recruiter, I hear every gripe from candidates and their countless frustrations with standard company hiring processes. Over-reliance on Applicant Tracking Systems and a lack of response or acknowledgement to applicants means you run the risk of missing a potential superstar. Put some control checks and contact points in along the way to maintain the 'human' element in the application process. This really helps you to sell your opportunities, starting with promoting your culture and the values of your organisation. It is vital that anyone you employ to represent your business, whether that is an in-house HR professional or your preferred agency partners, is capable of making a positive presentation to engage and motivate the talent.

Before you advertise, think! Companies around the world are guilty of overlooking their existing talent in their hasty assumption that there is no one within their organisation capable of fulfilling a particular role. Before you begin to fill the funnel from the top, ensure that your top employees aren't disappearing from the bottom. Lack of recognition and career development are two key reasons why organisations lose their vital staff. To look at it from another angle, how can you attract more talent into your organisation if you don't value the talent at your fingertips?! I've included some advice to improve employee retention in Section Five of this book. Of course, as a recruiter I would much rather you approach me to discuss filling a key vacancy, but if your staff turnover levels are high it affects my ability to attract talent into your organisation. A high turnover of staff is still very much a vital issue that requires immediate attention.

THE INTERVIEW

> *"I am a product of my circumstances, I am a product of my decisions."*
>
> *- Stephen Covey*

As a recruiter, one of the most common errors I see companies making more often than I would like is in failing to properly prepare for their interviews. Countless books have been written for candidates on how to prepare for interviews but there are few that advise hiring managers and employers on the process. This book isn't one either, I hasten to add, but we can at least cover the basics.

As the hiring manager/employer or person responsible for carrying out the interview, the onus is on you to leave the candidate with the overall impression of your company as being a great one to work for. Lack of interview preparation and research, negative body language, not having a copy of their CV with you – in fact all of the errors we berate candidates for and spend time as recruiters advising them on – these are all mistakes that employers are guilty of too!

If there's one thing to emphasise it is this:

FIRST IMPRESSIONS COUNT

As we have already seen – and I make no apology for repeating it yet again! – time and again surveys (and *Glassdoor!*) have shown that a poor interview experience will result in talented candidates leaving the interview process in droves.

One of those candidates could be that very superstar you have spent hours preparing your job advert for. While their encounter with your company does indeed start with the application process, a frustrating experience there can be overlooked if your advert, your company culture and the career development opportunities on offer compensate for it.

What no amount of backpedalling will make up for is a terrible experience at interview. *This is SUCH an important part of attracting and RETAINING your superstars, I can't emphasise it enough.*

Far too often in my recruitment career I've been faced with the frustration of an ideal candidate expressing doubts about an opportunity I've put them forward for, based on their experience at interview.

Your core values and culture are no more apparent than in an interview situation!

Now I've got that little matter out of the way (for now), let's focus on the interview itself.

My Top Three Interview Tips For Employers

I've lost count of the number of interviews I've carried out in my many years of recruiting.

What I have learnt is that focusing on a handful of points within your standard interview procedure will contribute towards a successful interview.

Let the candidate speak: Ask open questions that allow them to respond accordingly and share their achievements, their reasons for applying to this job and their long-term aspirations. Allow their personality to shine through. Avoid the temptation to ask closed questions that require only a 'yes' or 'no' answer.

Help them to relax: An anxious interviewee will never perform to the best of their ability. Some people are naturally nervous, regardless of how talented they are or how suited to the job they may be. Don't create an atmosphere. Be friendly yet professional, and avoid negative body language (don't sit with your head in your hands, or allow yourself to be distracted). Remember, technically speaking there are no wrong answers – the answers themselves will allow you to differentiate between suitable and unsuitable candidates.

Follow the same structure for each interview: Not only will this help you to compare each candidate on a level playing field, it will avoid any risk of bias or discrimination (see my note below).

A basic structure around which to develop your own interview strategy could take the following format:

- Encourage the candidate to tell you about their background and experience. Ask some non-competency-based questions. I've included forty of the most common non-competency-based questions in Appendix Three.

- Explore their CV, focusing on their experience and achievements relevant to the job.

- Outline what success looks like in this role and its key responsibilities.

- Focus on competency-based questions to drill down into their experience and ability. You will also find examples of competency-based questions to cover specific areas in Appendix Four. These are intended only as a guideline to enable you to generate your own ideas about what you may be able to use for your company, to adapt and adjust to meet your own criteria.

- Don't leave the candidate in any doubt as to what the job involves, and ensure that their expectations are realistic. If you don't get this aspect right during the interview stage, chances are that your ideal candidate will turn out to be a bad hire. Investment and time spent thoroughly assessing the candidate during the interview period will reap rewards further down the line AND avoid the potential for a bad hire. I really can't stress enough the negative impact a bad hire has on an organisation and again refer you to Appendix One where you will find more information on its effect and how to avoid it.

- Inform all candidates of the outcome of their interview where possible, and offer some constructive feedback as to why they were not successful. Nothing frustrates a candidate more than a standard "I'm sorry but your application was not successful on this occasion," especially for candidates who made it past the ATS, through the initial screening process and into the final round of interviews.

Oh – and one final huge tip – DON'T BE LATE!

It implies *disinterest* and a lack of respect – your superstar will run a mile.

A note on employment law

I am not a legal expert but have an awareness of the basics of employment law. As an employer you cannot discriminate against candidates based on their sex, race, age or disability. The interview process for every candidate should be uniform to avoid any potential for perceived discrimination. A competency-based interview process is ideal to avoid this problem.

I strongly advise that interview notes are kept on file to refer back to if needed. This is a requirement that you can be legally bound to. Having standardised interview questions to establish culture match should be straightforward and is relevant to every new employee. Getting into the habit of creating a job specification and advert before you start your search is critical. It is at this stage you should work out your standard interview questions for the vacancy. This makes your process uniform and traceable (just in case you ever need to refer back), but it also makes the process more efficient and appears more professional to candidates.

"If you're not willing to risk the unusual, you'll have to settle for the ordinary."

- Jim Rohn

THE COMMON TRAITS OF SUPERSTARS

As I touched upon earlier, it's not always what the candidate knows NOW – it's their FUTURE potential that matters.

Understanding that potential can help you, as an employer, in your quest to find the superstars you seek. Over the years I have learnt that the most intelligent brands evaluate an individual's potential for long-term success and especially ATTITUDE when selecting their preferred candidate.

I'll also let you in on a secret.

Regardless of industry, age, experience or anything else, the superstars you need to attract with your brand all share common traits. Here are just some of them – fifteen to be precise. You will undoubtedly have a few ideas of your own but my observations are based on working closely with employers across a variety of industry sectors and continually reviewing the career progress of the candidates I've placed over the years.

Your superstar will be:

Action-oriented: Superstars take chances, despite running the risk of failure. When they make mistakes they don't attempt to pass the buck but learn from them. Their mistakes often make them more successful and lead to new ideas. Employees who have never taken a risk won't bring the innovation you need to your brand – and they certainly won't be superstars.

Intelligent: While it's not the sole reason for hiring someone, intelligence provides strong foundations for future success. As an owner or manager in your company, you need someone who can work autonomously when required, rather than a team member who requires micromanaging. Guess who will be responsible for the micro-management...? That's right... YOU! (As if you haven't got enough to do already).

Ambitious: Superstars constantly seek to improve themselves and progress in their career. In doing that, they'll bring innovation and creativity to your company – and often inspire those around them to greater achievements.

A natural leader: If you cannot envisage a candidate playing a significant role or leading teams within your organisation, they are not superstars. Natural leaders exude confidence, treat those around them with courtesy and respect and enjoy continual success – which they also share with their teams. There's more to leadership than that of course, but we are focusing on hiring superstars in this book!

Autonomous: As a director, manager or owner of a company, you don't need to be handholding your new recruit. You need to be confident that the tasks you delegate to your new hire will be completed effectively, efficiently and on time. Autonomy comes naturally to superstars – they crave it!

A natural cultural fit: Can you envisage working with this candidate on a daily, weekly or monthly basis? Can you see them fitting in with your existing team? What does your instinct tell you? Cultural fit often means the difference between a great hire and a bad hire. These are crucial questions, especially for SMEs – superstars give you a distinct competitive advantage.

Positive and optimistic: Superstars are intrinsically upbeat. They generate a positive energy, which means people flock to them and thrive in their company. Taking challenges in their stride, the top talent helps to foster a working environment that encourages creativity and adds a spark to the working day. What's not to like?

Confident (but not arrogant): The most successful brands are confident in their ability to offer a superlative product or service and it's a confidence that permeates through their organisation. Guess where that confidence comes from? From the leadership AND the superstars at all levels of their organisation. Every superstar is confident; every superstar will help you to propel your business forward to where you want to be.

Honest: Integrity and authenticity are essential to achieve greatness in all walks of life. Your clients will be attracted by the candid nature of your organisation – and believe me, they can sense dishonesty a mile off. If your candidate isn't authentic and lacks integrity, they are not a superstar.

Successful: As a general rule, past performance predicts future behaviour. How long has the candidate remained in previous roles? Have they achieved, over-achieved or missed the boat? Scrutinise the CV of each individual closely – a lot can be gleaned from reading between the lines.

Focus on the detail: One thing I've learnt in my own career is that attention to detail is crucial to avoid errors that may jeopardise your company's reputation. Superstars are generally detail-oriented, ensuring all the 'i's are dotted and the 't's crossed. They ALWAYS get the job done.

Humble: Superstars allow their actions to speak for them. They don't need to be the big 'I am' or the permanent centre of attention. They know what's important, they understand what they need to do – and they do it. In my experience, the difference between confidence and arrogance is often the ability to be humble. Being humble enough to take other people's ideas on board, and spot talent that is often better then yourself, is a worthy trait to look out for in anyone.

Hard working: Achieving great things requires effort and going beyond the realms of normal working hours and traditional boundaries. There's no secret to success. As the great golfer Gary Player said, 'The harder I work, the luckier I get'. Superstars intuitively understand this and focus on hard work and achieving the results they seek. They are the lifeblood of every successful organisation. But then, you don't need me to tell you that. That's why you're reading this book, right?

Presentable: Top performers look the part. They are professional, well presented and well groomed. It's not about looks dictating success – it's about conforming to your brand image and representing your company in a professional, organised, respectful manner. The way in which candidates present themselves at interview can often be revealing. Superstars quite often dress for the 'next level up'.

PASSIONATE: Talented individuals love their job – they don't see it is as 'work' but as part of their life. As more Millennials infiltrate the workplace in the next decade, they will bring with them a sense of work/life integration rather than work/life balance. Your superstar will possess that same outlook.

Money will naturally always be a motivator but passionate employees, the superstars you seek, never 'work' a day in their life. They enjoy the journey and they are **always** confident of reaching their destination. This passion can often be seen by a person who demonstrates an ability to start early, finish later, work extra hours without being requested to do so, and remains positive and upbeat at all times. Ask about extra effort they have put in to complete projects and go above and beyond the basics.

This list is by no means exhaustive – and no doubt you will have your own views based on your experience. From my own observations, gained from working with numerous companies and candidates, however, I can say with a fair degree of confidence that these attributes are key indicators and high on the list of ways to identify superstar status.

A note on job-hoppers

Attitudes towards job-hoppers are changing, influenced by the growing presence of Generation Y in the workplace. When I first came into the recruitment sector, many employers would not consider a job-hopping candidate on the basis that past performance predicts future behaviour (in other words they wouldn't hang around for long).

I'm sure you're familiar with the phrase but for those that aren't, it describes a professional who frequently changes their job, literally switching from one employer to another. Job-hoppers typically stay in a role for two years at the most.

While the traditional employers' attitudes towards job-hoppers still prevails, attitudes are starting to shift – very slowly. Today's career isn't necessarily linear and many professionals are expected to change their jobs around half a dozen times before they reach 30.

Adam! I hear you say. *It's costly enough investing in new employees and finding superstars. Why would I want to consider a job-hopper?*

To be honest, I'm not saying you would, but in some industries, hiring a job-hopper can offer some benefits. I say this with caution and each case must be judged on its merits, but among the job-hopping candidates, you may just unearth your elusive superstar.

Job-hoppers often exhibit similar traits to superstars, which I've summarised below.

Firstly, job-hoppers **are often flexible and will take risks** (see my note on the 'action-oriented' trait of superstars above). In industries and organisations starved of talent, this can give your company a competitive edge.

At the same time, they **adapt quickly to different cultures,** bringing new perspectives into your company and an awareness of the strategies adopted by other organisations. Maybe they can bring a higher knowledge of your competitors and new ways to solve problems.

On top of that, one of the great advantages of job-hoppers is that they have normally **gained an extensive and impressive network** of contacts to bring to their new employer.

Your typical job-hopper is **not complacent**. They are habitually the 'new guy' or 'girl' on the block so need to be able to acclimatise quickly and hit the ground running. They crave quick successes and often command greater earning potential than their colleagues as they change jobs so frequently. *NB: The most successful job-hoppers always change roles 'upwards'*. Their high salaries are often justified by their achievements. Added to that is their ability to **continually learn new skills and hone those they already possess**. Job-hoppers, by their very nature, often remain at the peak of the game, taking the skills learnt in each role before they embrace new challenges.

Occasionally, **the job-hopper may just be the superstar your organisation needs**. The high achievers in many industries often move around more frequently than their peers as they are in demand for what they can bring to the table – if only for a short while. They are particularly suited to fast-paced industries such as IT.

In addition to the job market changing, I think it is only fair to consider the conditions of the wider economy. The period between 2008 and 2013 was incredibly volatile, with many hundreds of thousands of people being made redundant, and a number of them on multiple occasions. It would be unwise to discount candidates merely on the appearance that they were job-hoppers, and you should consider every case on merit and every candidate as an individual. This is the key to finding A-Player superstars to take your business forward.

The above scenarios, I know, will not be true of every job-hopping candidate but I stress again that the job-hopper of a decade ago is not the job-hopper we will see as the employment market continues to evolve in the next decade.

My recommendation is for all of us (including me!) to keep an open mind.

So, should you take a risk of your own and hire a job-hopper?

Again, I recommend that every individual is judged on their own merits and every decision to hire a candidate be considered against the changing face of the employment market and the needs of the business.

On a final note, Millennials are more likely to be among the job-hopping community, so my prediction is that employers' views of job-hopping candidates will ultimately change. How this impacts on the market and an employer's ability to retain its staff will be a challenge that every organisation will ultimately face.

I've provided more information on how to integrate Millennials into the workforce in Appendix Two.

Is Your Organisation Toxic?

Before we move on to consider additional interview tools or the scenario of making the offer and the counter offer, I want to highlight the signs of a toxic organisation. While it's intended to be tongue in cheek, the fact is that if you recognise your company in any of these descriptions, you are probably failing to attract the superstars you are in search of – and if you are managing to recruit them, you must have something exceptional!

Communication: Your communication with candidates is either unprofessional or verging on disrespectful. You repeatedly reschedule interviews and your receptionist is rude and sullen. As the interviewer, you sit back in your chair, gaze distractedly around the room, aren't interested in a word the candidate has to say and frequently put your head in your hands.

You ignore the candidate's questions: Ignorance isn't acceptable. Even if you don't know the answer to a question, or can't answer for confidentiality reasons, at least make an effort. Candidates deserve to know the likely timeline for the interview process and why the job is vacant, whether you feel obliged to tell them or not.

There's a cloud of doom hanging over your office: How often do your employees smile? What's the ambience like as you walk through your offices? If your employees avoid eye contact and refuse to acknowledge visitors with a smile, you've got problems – and your candidates will know it. Imagine spending eight hours a day, five days a week in a negative environment… if you don't have to imagine, I refer you again to the Section Two of the book!

You haven't got a job description: It happens. Companies don't always have job descriptions, especially when they get the chance to interview a superstar out of the blue. That's acceptable because, after all, exceptional talent deserves exceptional circumstances. If, however, you don't possess a job description because HR simply haven't got round to producing one yet, what on earth were you doing advertising the job? A savvy candidate will see straight through your lack of organisation and commitment to the HR processes and that's probably the last you'll see of them.

Your hiring manager/interviewer criticises your company/employees: Don't dismiss this as impossible. Have you participated in your hiring process recently? If you hiring manager isn't happy, your interviewees will know it.

For companies struggling to attract or retain talent, it's possible that your organisation is exhibiting toxic signs during the hiring process.

ADDITIONAL RECRUITMENT TOOLS

As I mentioned at the opening of this book, it is SO important to follow your gut instinct when you meet prospective employees. Having said that, when you are desperate to find talent, sometimes you may need some perspective and formal confirmation that your intuition is guiding you properly.

One of my favourite principles is this – THROW AWAY THE DESK!

Why would you hire someone you have only seen across a desk? Get them to stand on their own two feet, literally. Give them the opportunity to show you just who they are and what they are capable of.

Two great ways of doing this, which supplement the competency-based interview, are through assessment centres and psychometric tests.

Assessment Centres

Using an assessment centre is a fairly common recruitment technique that involves assessing candidates through a series of group exercises. Assessment centres are often used in graduate recruitment or for roles that require a degree of teamwork. Typically, they are used by larger employers such as public sector organisations, large retailers, banks, financial institutions and service companies, particularly in the IT sector.

It's a little bit like the TV show Big Brother, where the housemates attempt to project a certain persona when they walk into the house that later falls apart as we see the true character behind the façade.

Gradually, your candidates will reveal the true person behind the mask, rather than just putting on an act for an hour in a traditional desk based interview. 'Ice breakers', coffee breaks and lunchtimes are the ideal situations to see the true character. Fans of Sir Alan Sugar's TV programme The Apprentice will know exactly what I am talking about. How long before they forget the cameras are permanently on them? Doesn't it make great TV!

SMEs don't generally have a need to put their candidates through the rigours of a group exercise as they are quite expensive to run, but you can still adopt the same principles within a scaled-down setting.

Assessment centres – or group exercises – are generally run over one or two days, depending on the level of the position or the number of vacancies up for grabs. In terms of sequence, they usually happen after the initial screening process of ATS and possibly telephone screening, and often combine face-to-face interviews on the day.

The Advantages of Group Exercises

As an employer, a group exercise will allow you to gain a more thorough understanding of the interpersonal skills of candidates. That is, how they react to working in a team and their ability to perform under pressure. Some of us naturally step back when faced with a team environment, while some of us will attempt to dominate and lead. How we respond in these situations reflects whether or not we will fit into an employer's culture.

Group exercises are fascinating to observe and can help you to identify a potential superstar in your group of candidates. For larger organisations they are especially effective and the advantages of using them include the following:

- Statistics suggest that they are the most dependable method of evaluating a candidate's suitability for a position, as they are assessed on their response to a number of different group situations. Some surveys indicate that they provide the employer with a 60% accuracy rate of candidate suitability, compared to a rate of around 15% for recruitment via interviewing alone. *In other words, they help you to spot the top talent quickly and effectively!*

- Group exercises are selected to allow candidates to demonstrate as broad a range of skills as possible.

- In most industry sectors, they are regarded as a fair reflection of candidate ability as well as the most in-depth way of assessing applicants based on merit.

- They are practical. Group exercises are based on practice, not simply theory, and for larger companies this can be far more effective than interviews.

- Group exercises give your superstars the opportunity to shine! They offer candidates the chance to demonstrate how they will perform if selected for a particular role, not solely how well they perform in interview.

SMEs can adopt the principles of assessment centres and apply them to a smaller group setting.

I've used similar ideas when recruiting my own team to great effect and also advised, designed and facilitated group assessment centres for hundreds of SMEs, even some start-up one-man bands. It always gives greater confidence in the hiring/decision-making process. The hirer knows who they are getting in much more detail and can decide if they would like to work with the new starter to build their business. So take my advice and, wherever possible, throw away the desk!

Psychometric Tests

Psychometric tests (also known as personality or aptitude tests) reveal a lot more about the individual's hidden character and often disclose surprising information, not only about what drives them but their preferred style of working.

Over three quarters of The Times' Top 100 Companies in the UK use them in the hiring processes, so on that basis I would say they are fairly effective! My favourite psychometric tests are offered by Thomas International but a number of companies offer different styles of testing.

The different types of psychometric tests include:

- Verbal and non-verbal reasoning

- Numerical reasoning

- Personality questionnaires

- Logical reasoning.

Unlike assessment centres, they are much more affordable for smaller businesses. They help to reinforce your initial opinion (or otherwise!) of a candidate, and they're great value for money.

The Advantages Of Psychometric Tests

Psychometric tests are impersonal, standardised and objective, offering you, the employer additional insights into what really goes on in the mind of your potential superstar. What's more, they are unbiased, assessing candidates on an equal footing. Psychometric tests are oblivious to skills, qualifications and experience, providing objective assessments of the strengths and weaknesses of your candidates.

We can all turn on the charm in an interview and put on a display of our best behaviour, but psychometric tests blow any illusion your candidates attempt to present out of the water.

Depending on your requirements, you can use psychometric tests at various stages of the hiring process:

- As an online screening tool for volume applications

- As part of the first interview

- As part of an overall assessment centre day

- During a final interview, particularly for a senior role where the risks of getting it wrong can be the most detrimental.

My advice is, *don't rely solely on psychometric tests in the final candidate selection – take into account all of the 'evidence' you gather from competency-based interviews, group exercises and reference checks.*

I've seen instances where the best candidate has somehow performed badly on a psychometric test. Fortunately, the employer believed they had potential and still appointed them – and they are still doing an outstanding job to this day.

Reference Checks

Your final tool in your search for a superstar is, of course, the good old-fashioned reference check. I am still amazed at the number of employers who don't carry out these checks in their haste to appoint a potential superstar. If you're one of them, you may want to consider these statistics from a further *CareerBuilder* survey:

- 20% of employers did not carry out reference checks prior to making a job offer

- Of those that did, 69% changed their mind about a candidate's suitability for a vacancy based on the feedback they received

- 62% of references reflected negatively on the candidate

- 29% revealed the presence of misleading information on a candidate's CV.

You know what I'm going to say.

Always carry out reference checks!

THE JOB OFFER

Firstly, A Few Tips On Improving Your Job Offer

One concern expressed, particularly by the smaller businesses I work with, is how they can possibly compete with the 'big boys' to whom money is no object. In truth, smaller companies often offer superstars a great opportunity to shine and achieve their objectives, as there are no restrictive company structures to overcome.

Even within the fairly flat structure of an SME, business owners enjoy a flexibility that larger organisations simply don't have and can create opportunities for their top talent.

Yes, I hear you cry, *BUT how can we compete on salary?*

In all honesty, you probably can't when push comes to shove... BUT...

As well as a basic salary, you may want to consider the following:

Remember, money is only one motivator for superstars and it's rarely the prime motivator. Culture, leadership and career-development opportunities all feature highly on the 'tick list' of the top performers.

Also, I regularly see senior managers in larger organisations who have lost their belief in what the corporation they work for stands for. They have a comfortable level of earnings, and usually a degree of financial security, and so you can attract them into your business if you really sell (and believe in!) what you as an individual and business stand for. Again, referring to Simon Sinek's *'Start with WHY'*, you should find your own 'WHY' and shout it from the rooftops. Not only will you attract countless new customers, but you will also have an army of people desperate to get on your bus. Your 'WHY' has to be strong though, and of course you have to believe it from your core.

Additionally, try these suggestions if you're stuck on how to improve your offer and lure the talent you really want:

Flexible working hours: Work/life balance is THE number one benefit you can offer candidates. It's also one of the easiest ways of improving your offer. Can you offer the opportunity to work from home or flexi-time around core hours to your best employees? *Can you afford not to if you want to recruit the superstars?*

Contributions towards the daily commute: This doesn't mean the expense of a company car, unless it's justified within the responsibilities of the job. Offer a contribution towards a rail ticket or a car allowance where feasible. In the final evaluation, from your favourite candidate's viewpoint it all helps.

More holidays: Another 'work/life balance' option is to include an extra day or two of annual leave in your job offer. No one can work at perpetual full speed without some time out to reflect and rejuvenate. The extra days in an employee's annual entitlement really do make a difference. After all, you don't want your superstars burnt out. So, what's it to be? An extra day or two of holiday, or a week off with exhaustion?

Help with childcare: Childcare costs in the UK are among the most prohibitive in Europe. Can you offer vouchers or contributions to offset these often onerous costs?

Healthcare: If you can – or do – offer healthcare to your employees only, explore the possibility of extending it to family members at corporate rates (payable by your employee). It's a small gesture, but often an effective one.

Career development: The top talent in every organisation is constantly seeking new ways to expand their knowledge base and gain new qualifications. Countless surveys by companies like Deloitte and PwC show that the opportunity for career development is essential to attract high achievers to your organisation. Again, my question to you is, can you afford not to?

These are only a few suggestions on how to improve your overall job offer. SMEs also have the advantage of being able to adopt a 'mix and match' approach to individual job offers and can tailor their final proposal to their chosen candidate.

Its yet another vital tactic in your quest to find superstars!

And Finally... The Counter Offer

You've carried out your screening, asked the competency-based questions, implemented a psychometric test, observed your top candidates in group exercises and created the best job offer you can afford – *now you have to overcome the possibility of the counter offer!*

(WHERE DOES IT ALL END?)

Yes, your long journey towards appointing your superstar isn't quite over yet.

Ultimately, there's nothing much you can do about candidates who accept a counter offer and it isn't always an increase in salary that changes your superstar's mind. The one advantage that you have is that there is something that prompted them to explore your opportunity – *ergo,* there is something missing in their current job.

As a recruiter, I know that accepting a counter offer is generally a mistake on the part of the candidate. Initially, it's flattering, but in my experience, those same candidates who accept counter offers are looking for a move again within six months. As I already mentioned, it isn't all about money.

If you are working with a recruiter, the counter-offer scenario should be covered early on in the candidate-assessment process. That's not to say that it doesn't still happen, but it is less common. So, what can you do if you are dealing directly with a candidate?

Anticipate The Counter Offer

For companies working directly, include the following questions in your interview process, as early on as you can:

- Why are you unhappy in your current position? Have you addressed this issue with your employer and if so how did they respond?

- If we offer you this job, what are the chances of you receiving a counter offer from your current employer? How will you respond to this offer? If it is purely a monetary offer, how will you feel in six months' time?

- What would make you stay with your current employer?

- If you would not accept a counter offer, why not?

- Do you really want to leave your current position?

Ultimately, as frustrating as it may be, see it as a positive move if the candidate accepts a counter offer. Generally, it means they can be bought. While it's frustrating at the time, it is much better for your organisation than the cost, in every way, of a bad hire.

It also gives you the chance to find someone who is genuinely interested in your opportunity and your company for the right reasons! Someone that believes your 'WHY' as strongly as you do.

We've taken a long ride through the hiring process but all we've done is dipped our toe in the shallow end. Each section we've covered would merit a book all of its own and you will no doubt approach each element differently based on your own organisation's needs and culture.

What I've provided in this section is a blueprint and a guideline for you to build upon for the future – a map to help you navigate towards those superstars.

Having said that, the journey is never-ending! In the next section I'll explain why, when it comes to superstars, you should ALWAYS BE LOOKING!

"I'm here 24 7 in case opportunity calls when I least expect HER to"

SECTION FOUR: ALWAYS BE LOOKING

"If you can hire people whose passion intersects with the job, they won't require any supervision at all. They will manage themselves better than anyone could ever manage them. Their fire comes from within, not from without. Their motivation is internal, not external."

- Stephen Covey

The search for your superstar isn't an occasional strategy you adopt when you have a vacancy within your company. My advice to all employers and business owners I work with when asked how to resolve their issues over attracting the right talent is this:

DON'T EVER STOP SEARCHING FOR TALENT

This seems so obvious but you should always be looking for the talent that can take you to where you want to be. You should be constantly thinking about your long-term plan, and how you are going to recruit for it.

I always look ahead at least six months and sometimes even 12 when it comes to talent and seeking out superstars.

I am constantly aware of the skills I need in my business and keep in close contact with those people in my network who may be able to help me find them.

It pays dividends to build relationships of trust and respect with your potential superstars so that when the time is right to move you can push the button and get them on board quickly!

Responding to short-term trends is a recipe for failure.

The key to finding, hiring and KEEPING your superstars requires a long-term strategy aligned with your succession planning. Don't just take my word for it. In its survey of over 2,000 executives in 2013, The Boston Consulting Group revealed that between 60% to 80% of the top European leaders are promoted internally – *but here's the rub.*

It takes around ten years for the top talent to reach those senior-level roles.

Successful companies – the type of company you want to build – plan their talent needs FIVE YEARS AHEAD!

So let's consider the ways in which you can continually look for talent and build up your own TALENT PIPELINE!

WORD OF MOUTH (BEGIN FROM WITHIN)

Let's build on the point that I raised above. There is no better place to start than with your existing team members. They are the ones who know what it's like to work within your organisation and they know what management style works well. They know what a cultural fit looks like for you.

Build your 'Star Player' mentality and encourage it across your organisation.

Let all of your employees and network of contacts know that you are ALWAYS interested in meeting exceptional people.

Hire the talent when you see it, even if you don't have a job opening – your trust in them will pay dividends.

Implement an employee-referral programme. For a growing number of companies, employee referrals have become a critical component in their efforts to attract the top talent they need.

As a generalisation, employee referrals provide better-than-average candidates.

My questions to you are:

How are you using the power of your network to increase your talent pipeline?

What would you offer an employee as an incentive to refer talent? Is it on a par with what you might pay a recruitment agency who may not always grasp your culture as well as an existing team member? If not, then why not?

What process do you have to ask your existing talent pipeline to refer you to other quality candidates?

When it comes to offering financial rewards and incentives, never under-estimate the potential for finding – and hiring – some great talent. If your core values are aligned with your company culture (and I refer you all the way back to Section Two on culture yet again here) your employees should really WANT to help you bring more talent on board.

It is to everyone's advantage after all.

The simple act of asking for recommendations from your existing staff can point you to some exceptional talent who will fit well within your organisation. My only caveat is – it's probably not a great idea to employ an employee's 'best mate' if they are going to be working closely together.

I'm sure you don't need me to explain to you my reasoning behind this advice.

DATABASE

It's probably the most obvious point I can make in building your talent pipeline. When it comes to recruitment (as I should know) the biggest asset in your business is your database.

Are you serious about building your business?

Are you serious about finding and keeping great people?

In that case, I urge you to start thinking like a recruiter and start to build your database of potential future talent **RIGHT NOW!**

When it comes down to it, professional recruiters are obsessive about maintaining an up-to-date database of all the movers and shakers in their industry. I should know. I'm one of those obsessives.

For every single candidate that comes through our business, we 'keyword' each one so than we understand exactly what their skills are. As well as that, we note their character traits during our last conversation with them.

Why database? It's quite simple. It means we can stay in touch regularly with the talent we might need for future opportunities. More than that, through constantly networking with them, we often find that they are also excellent sources for additional referrals.

If you haven't got a database, or the one you have is in desperate need of some TLC, I seriously recommend you begin work on it today. To get you up and running, get in touch with one of my team who can set you up on the free ATS that we offer to our clients. Failing that, just search for Applicant Tracking Systems (ATS) in Google and see what it throws up.

You'll be amazed.

There are hundreds of systems available, many offering the opportunity for a free trial which allows you to experiment with a few and work out what complements your HR strategies and recruitment needs.

WIDEN YOUR NET

This stage represents the third of my '3 Ms' – **MEDIA**, specifically SOCIAL MEDIA**.

If you recall:

Once you understand your vision of the superstars you want to attract, you need to begin looking. As I stated earlier, engagement with talented performers begins long before the formal hiring process starts. Now is the time to engage with media in all of its forms, press releases, job boards, trade press and especially SOCIAL MEDIA – to engage with your future superstars.

Let's see how.

Firstly, there will come a time in every hiring policy when all of your strategic thinking and word of mouth/networking efforts are not yielding the calibre of candidates that you need to propel your business forward.

This is the time you need to widen the net.

By widening the net, I mean the use of social networks and job boards.

Job boards: Unbelievably, there are now in excess of 3,000 job boards in the UK, covering every industry, job and location you can possibly imagine. It's impossible for me to say which job boards would work best for your particular industry, so it's essential to do your research. Ask for statistics from the jobsites themselves on website traffic before committing to a paid membership. A number of them will offer you a free trial, which I would highly recommend as it is an excellent way of assessing their suitability for your industry sector and the talent you are in search of.

According to my own research (carried out on my database of over 140,000 job seekers) *over 90% of people start their search online these days*. Remember the figures we talked about through mobile job searches alone?

In my personal opinion – for what it's worth – it is essential to direct your focus in this area. Steer clear of expensive and (in my experience) often ineffective newspaper adverts. They are generally pointless and, in the majority of cases, the talent you seek can be discovered for significantly less investment in terms of time and money.

Social media: Let's get this straight. In this day and age, building your online presence in an effective manner that reflects your core values and company culture in an on-going basis is essential in order to attract the superstars you need.

In this day and age, the obvious place to begin to build an online presence is through your own social networks. Here are my golden rules for building your online presence effectively.

Understand your own message: Before you launch, review or hone your online presence, you must get the message you want to convey clear in your own mind. What do you have that your competition doesn't? What image do your currently portray online? Whatever that message is, it MUST be consistent and it MUST reflect your core values and culture. (Yes, we're back to Section Two on culture again!)

Decide on your network of choice: Which social media outlet is most appropriate to attract your target audience? *LinkedIn* is an obvious first choice. It's today's equivalent of the Rolodex (do you remember Rolodex?). Unlike the Rolodex, *LinkedIn* is never out of date. Forget the business cards: for an instant update on the job status of your connections, just check out their *LinkedIn* profile. Staying in touch has never been so easy. Take advantage of the Advanced Search facility on *LinkedIn* to find the potential talent in your chosen location who possess the EXACT skills you are looking for. Once you find them, it's so easy to connect with them and BEGIN TO ENGAGE!

Twitter and *Facebook* are two more obvious choices. I'll let you into a secret now. A simple status update on *Facebook* has landed me a placement fee of £6,500 in the past so it's got to be worth a try. When it comes to *Twitter*, if you have any kind of profile, be bold – broadcast what you are looking for.

Ask for re-tweets, offer incentives for followers who can point you in the direction of future talent and ENGAGE! Enter into a conversation, ask questions, re-tweet or share status updates of others.

Don't ignore Google+: Once you get the hang of it, you have another outlet for your job search. Its users are typically the younger tech-savvy professionals – the Millennials. What's more, it's Google – which means a presence on Google+ is guaranteed to boost your search engine ranking. Yet again – and at the risk of sounding like a member of the Star Trek cast – you must ENGAGE!

A company blog also offers a great way of keeping your website up to date and of obtaining the personal email addresses of your subscribers. Don't dismiss *YouTube* either – many of the big (and smaller) brands enjoy viral success with their recruiting videos. *Twitter* is just one of them!

Regular postings: The reason I highlighted 'selecting your network of choice' in the previous point is that every account needs regular attention – that's regular posts, status updates and a consistency of new articles and links for a blog. A *LinkedIn* company page or *Twitter* feed that hasn't been updated in three weeks implies that a company doesn't understand the power of social recruiting.

Take a look at what your most successful competitors are doing and learn from them. The most visible and successful brands provide regular content and listen to the feedback from their audience. If it just isn't practical to run several social media accounts at this stage in your organisation's development select the most important one (*hint: it's usually LinkedIn*) and put all of your efforts into it. You won't regret it.

Show, don't tell: If you have to TELL candidates why they should apply to your company, you're doing it wrong. If you have a clearly defined brand and confident culture, this should be reflected in regular and positive engagement with your audience, coupled with relevant articles and updated blog posts. At this stage, you should be reeling the talent in slowly yet consistently without them knowing anything about it!

I have two final rules for your online activity, which have proved invaluable to me:

1. BE PATIENT! Don't expect overnight miracles. Consistency, persistence and perseverance are the keys to long-term success online. Use tools such as Google Analytics to assess your progress and DON'T GIVE UP!

2. ENGAGE! Engage with your audience regularly. Take on board any feedback and up your game. Tomorrow's talent is online and looking for a company that matches up to their long-term career aspirations. Make sure it's yours!

The social media landscape is just like the real world – the more you give the more you get.

I often look at social media like a cocktail party (I don't attend many 'cocktail parties' and I'm sure you don't either, but go with the analogy here!) The people you meet at parties broadly split into two categories: the ones you enjoy meeting and the ones that you don't.

The people you don't enjoy meeting are the rude ones. They are the ones that talk about themselves endlessly (how great they are or - God forbid - how great their kids are!!!), who are inconsiderate of your personal space (too loud or too quiet), and who often express poorly thought-out views that offend on levels of race, religion or politics. They definitely don't remember your name, mainly because they didn't ask in the first place, but they were very keen to tell you theirs. My rule of thumb is that the only people really, really interested in you are 1) you and 2) if you're lucky, your mum.

No one else is that interested, but these people don't know that. We've all suffered them, and wish we hadn't!

The people that you enjoy meeting and would like to meet again are very different. They ask questions and are genuinely interested in your response, even if you talk about your kids! They get your name and remember it first time without being prompted. They respond to your questions and find common ground for discussion, and they don't impose their views or ways of thinking on you. Often they are funny, and generally they attract others into a group.

And so it is online, in the world of social media. Create dialogue, be interested, be interesting, be friendly, give not to receive, be funny (appropriately), be yourself and create dialogue that is a two-way conversation of equal measure.

People will be drawn to you, and refer others to share your message and way of thinking. Superstar talent will automatically want to find out more.

WORK WITH A RECRUITER WHO UNDERSTANDS YOUR MARKET

OK, so I'm predictable. Of course I would suggest you work with a recruiter, but specialist recruiters WHO UNDERSTAND YOUR MARKET AND YOUR NICHE can save you time and money as well as reduce the potential risk of a BAD HIRE!

When you know how to work with a recruiter, you expand your potential talent pipeline, but to do this you MUST work with a recruiter who understands your market.

Use recruiters – build relationships, let them know the type of talent you want so they contact you FIRST the minute that talent surfaces in their searches.

Five Golden Rules for Working with a Recruiter

Firstly, be sure you are fully committed to the hiring process: As a recruiter I am approached by too many clients who tell me they are committed to the hiring process but when it comes to it, they are difficult to contact, don't review CVs quickly and continually postpone interviews.

Know your job description inside out: You need to know the performance objectives of the vacancy inside out – information you will be able to draw from your job description and performance criteria. Understand what success looks like in this role and be prepared to consider future potential rather than relying solely on current experience. Make sure your recruitment partner also has this level of detail.

Interview all of the shortlist: A recruiter who understands your niche will present pre-qualified candidates – the 'best available' talent rather than the 'most visible' you will encounter on every jobsite. That's what you pay a recruiter for.

On top of that, a specialist, reputable agency will ensure that every single candidate on that shortlist meets the essential criteria from your performance based job description.

Be available and be present: You MUST be fully engaged with all of the candidates presented through your recruiter. As a rule of thumb, you are more likely to meet with 'passive' candidates this way. By that, I mean candidates who aren't desperately seeking their next move but WILL consider a move to a company that can offer them opportunities that meet their aspiration. You MUST fully invest in the interview process if you want to attract top talent and ensure acceptance of your job offer. I know I have said this early in this chapter but it bears repeating.

The buck stops with you: While a specialist recruiter will provide high-calibre candidates who have been background checked, the ultimate responsibility for candidate selection and formal reference checks lies with the employer (YOU!).

At the end of the day, a specialist recruiter saves you time, reduces the risk of a bad hire and – most importantly – RAISES THE TALENT BAR WITHIN YOUR COMPANY! So now you are beginning to grasp the basics of how and where to constantly be seeking out superstars, we return to the final problem of KEEPING THEM ONCE YOU HAVE HIRED THEM!

A GOOD EMPLOYEE IS ALWAYS PUNCTUAL!

SECTION FIVE: RETAINING YOUR SUPERSTARS

As if it isn't a big enough challenge finding and hiring your superstars, now we come to the next challenge.

Keeping them within your company!

Get Onboard!

So now we come to *on-boarding* – the process that allows your new employees to quickly integrate within your organisation. You would be amazed at how many companies we've worked with over the years that literally hand out their new hire's login information on day one and leave them to make it up as they go along.

In case you haven't realised – this is not the way to retain your talent!

First of all, don't be in any doubt: the first three months of every new hire's tenure are the most crucial and their experiences during that time represent the difference between them staying and going.

Here are my top tips for what you, as a responsible employer, should be doing to integrate them successfully into your organisation.

Build anticipation

The time from the acceptance of a job offer to starting in a new career can seem like an eternity for your employee-to-be. A typical notice period is around a month. This is your chance to build the excitement and anticipation so they come to you hungrier than ever to make an impact.

Keep in contact throughout that period – write to them with information on what's currently happening, express how keen you are to have them on board and let them know who they will be working with. Provide them with as much information as possible to maintain that excitement.

Adopt a 'hands on' approach

Add a human touch to their early days. Don't dump them in a corner with your company manual. Work through the manual with them - that requires face-to-face contact by the way. On-boarding systems that involve human interaction improve levels of employee satisfaction, retention and performance.

You've invested in this superstar and you need a return on this investment. Start how you mean to go on!

Start from the top

Most of us are more alert and receptive to new information at the beginning of the day or on-boarding programme. Include your most important elements at the outset for maximum effect.

Encourage communication

One-on-one updates with a line manager who is both approachable and acknowledges early successes will ensure smooth integration of your newly acquired superstar into your company. When new hires fail it is often because their boss is a remote and aloof figure. Your superstars need – and want – to know what's expected of them and where they fit into YOUR big picture. Give them the tools, goals and support they need and watch them soar!

Put your managers in key on-boarding positions

This will allow them to be fully involved in your new hire's experience. Your managers should understand what's expected of them, as well as what's expected of your new employee.

Keep it simple and straightforward

Too much information/introductions/details will overwhelm even your brightest superstar. Pace your on-boarding programme carefully to keep it interesting and enable your new starter to absorb all of the essential details. Mix policies and procedures with some interaction with their new colleagues before moving on to their personal responsibilities for maximum effect. Trust me, it works.

Use a mentoring or buddy system

Employee retention levels are generally higher in companies that appoint an experienced employee to act as a mentor for your new talent. That way, any potential issues can be quickly identified and resolved while reducing the risk of anxiety for your new starter.

Set achievable goals

Superstars need to achieve and they need to achieve quickly. Set them objectives that can be met early on in their new role to give them some early 'wins'. Let them know you value them and regard them as an essential member of the team. That way, they'll want to stay with your company.

Keep it up!!

The top talent need continual recognition so don't allow the communication lines to close after the on-boarding process draws to an end.

This is where employee engagement comes in ...

PLAYING FOR KEEPS

The days of a 'job for life' and the gold carriage clock awarded for forty years of service are long gone, and I personally don't see that as a bad thing in the slightest!

Sooner or later, members of your team may leave you, but you shouldn't take it too personally – although I do recommend an exit interview to ascertain their reasons.

Ninety percent of the time, however, you should see it as an opportunity to bring in some fresh talent!

As you will know by now, I'm a big believer that if you get your message right and set the expectations from the beginning (which goes back yet again to where we started, examining your core values and your culture) then your chances of retaining your top talent will dramatically increase – which leads me to...

The secrets of employee retention.

Well, they aren't secrets but the attitude of some employers towards engaging and retaining their talent sometimes makes me wonder if they are even remotely aware of the basic principles of employee retention.

Here are my top tips to help you to improve your chances of retaining the superstar you just hired.

Number One: Engage Your Employees

In 2013, Gallup carried out a State Of The Workplace poll in the US. Where the US goes, we generally follow in our employment trends. That poll of 150,000 workers showed that 70% felt they were 'not engaged' with their managers. Some went so far as to declare themselves 'actively disengaged.'

Even with my basic maths skills, I calculate that to mean that only 30% of the workforce was engaged. If we face similar statistics, what kind of impact does that have on the day-to-day productivity of your employees? Coming closer to home, a Hay Group survey revealed that 94% of employees believe their efforts to engage with their teams have resulted in a distinct improvement in their talent retention strategy. To stand any chance of retaining your superstars, you MUST ENGAGE with them!

Number Two: Sing Their Praises, Recognise Their Achievements

Under-estimate or under-utilise this advice at your peril! I know you are busy, I know you are stressed and I know that you care far more about your business than anyone else ever will BUT!!!.... you MUST take the time to recognise your employees for a job well done. We all want hard-working people, right? Well, the way to get them to work hard is to express your gratitude when it's due. Lack of recognition for their achievements consistently ranks highly on the surveys of why employees leave their jobs. Larger companies might want to go so far as to establish a formal employee recognition policy to retain their key players. Take it from me, a simple 'thank you' goes a long way and motivates your staff to work harder. It also helps to retain your top talent.

Number Three: On-Going Skills And Career Development

Don't take my word for it. As I mentioned very early on in this book, Deloitte's Human Capital Trends report, issued in 2013, predicted a move from the war to recruit talent to one of 'developing' talent. If you haven't got an employee development programme in place, it may be time to consider one. That's if you're serious about attracting and retaining superstars to your company, of course.

Number Four: Employee Surveys

If the chapter on culture and core values didn't prompt you to consider an employee survey, then perhaps this will. It is an effective way of identifying issues with motivation in your teams as well as a great way of building team morale and trust. You NEED to know the view of your employees on teamwork, leadership, your vision for the company, the vital issue of work/life balance and what they think about opportunities for career progression. The information you glean from this exercise may not be what you WANT to know, but that is an entirely different matter. If you're hesitant about carrying out employee surveys then we both know there is a problem with your retention levels.

Number Five: Leadership

It really does start at the top. You know it and I know it. Poor leadership leads to reduced productivity, higher staff turnover, employees going AWOL and low levels of employee engagement. Your leadership should reflect your culture and values and if you get that right you'll find that your talent will be happy to stay with you.

Number Six: Interact With Your Teams

Don't hang around waiting for the next performance review. Encourage daily and open communication between managers and their teams (or you and your employees in a smaller business). Maintain an 'open door' policy, set up an employee suggestion scheme and encourage your talent to approach you with their concerns. When you go to the office tomorrow, ask your employees if they can describe your company vision. If they can't, it's time for a change in the way you communicate. Be brave!

Number Seven: Money and Incentives

Cash is an obvious incentive when it comes to retaining your high achievers. Who doesn't love a big fat pay packet at the end of each month? Wherever possible, I urge you to tie in the success of the individual with the success of your business.

Include bonus payments (and consider shares/equity options for your senior teams) as key elements of your incentives in the company. Nothing motivates employees more than to know they have a share in your/their business. As we've seen, however, it's not all about money.

One of the major motivations for my own team is the fact that the people on target for their Key Performance Indicators all qualify for extra annual leave, and if we hit target there is always a paid-for drinks party on the last Friday of the month. I'll tell you now – that focuses the mind of everyone in the business to get to and beat their KPIs, personally and as a group.

Number Eight: Have Some Fun!

We know what happens to Jack (and Jill) when it's all work and no play. As Generation Y takes over the workplace, the more successful employers will learn to offer more autonomy and encourage innovation. It's guaranteed to lighten up a staid office and bring some fun back into the working week.

Hiring A SuperStar

"If you go to work on your goals, your goals will go to work on you. If you go to work on your plan, your plan will go to work on you. Whatever good things we build end up building us."

- Jim Rohn

SUMMARY

So there you have it.

The nuts and bolts of the whole hiring process, gained from the pains and gains of many years spent in the beguiling, rewarding and occasionally frustrating world of recruitment – or talent acquisition as you may now know it.

Whatever you prefer to call it, once you understand the fundamental principles of the hiring process, you will begin to discover, attract and retain the superstars you've needed for so long to achieve your vision for your business (and for yourself).

Here's to your future superstars – and your life-long success!

If you have any recruitment stories of your own you would like to share, or have any questions for Adam and his team go to www.adambutlerltd.co.uk or email adamb@adambutler.co.uk

"Whatever the mind can conceive and believe, it can achieve."

- Napoleon Hill

APPENDIX ONE

EMPLOYMENT COSTS AND THE COST OF A BAD HIRE

A lot of businesses I speak to are generally focused with two key metrics – namely 'time to hire' and the 'cost of hire'.

Surely, anyone who is serious about attracting superstars into their business should focus on the quality of talent regardless of cost? The best talent will always repay your investment in double-quick time by either saving or making MORE MONEY!

If you are looking for a sales person, you need to know how much revenue they will bring in to your company. If a new sales person generates £250,000 of sales, of which £125,000 was net profit, it doesn't take a genius to work out that it would be worth investing more into finding them in the first place, does it?

The return on investment for paying a recruitment agency fee, for example would pale into insignificance.

For example:

Sales target for new sales person - £250,000

Sales person salary - £25,000

Sales commission when at target - £25,000

Cost of sales (including stock, services, overheads) - £100,000

Recruitment agency fee (20% of 1st year salary) - £5,000

Total Costs - £155,000

Total profit for your business from a £5,000 fee - <u>£95,000!</u>

You know it makes sense.

The cost of getting it wrong, however, is another matter entirely.

Figures released in February 2014 suggests the cost of a replacing an employee who is leaving your company is £30,614 (calculated by Oxford Economics).

General estimates of the cost of a bad hire range from one third of a new hire's first-year salary to FIVE TIMES their first-year salary. FIVE TIMES! It doesn't bear thinking about.

To make matters worse, the Harvard Business Review suggests that *80% of all staff turnover is a direct consequence of poor hiring decisions.*

When you think about it, a company doesn't just lose time and the financial investment when an employee doesn't work out. Hiring the wrong person can lead to poor customer service, lower team morale and a bunch of disaffected employees who are left to pick up the pieces.

No wonder so many hiring managers are accused of taking their time making a decision when the cost of getting it wrong is sky high in so many ways!

As technological advances continue to affect recruitment strategies, I regularly deal with pressured HR departments and business owners who feel that they MUST complete tasks faster and with more efficiency than ever before. This includes bringing on their new employees.

So what can you do to minimise the risk of your next hire being a bad one?

Firstly, you have to **understand what's needed**. Go right back to the job description (yet again). Review what sector trends have changed since you last filled this vacancy. Decide what success looks like in this job. Check, check and check again that this is reflected in your job description. You MUST understand thoroughly the type of candidate you need and if you are unsure – DON'T proceed with the hiring process until you DO!

Create a detailed hiring plan that explains who will be involved in recruiting for this role and at what stage. Look at what went wrong with your last bad hire and put checks in place to ensure it DOESN'T happen again. Agree how long it will take to arrange interviews and the response time to candidates in between each interview. Review your on-boarding process. Consider working with a recruiter who understands your requirements and has access to the talent you need (yes, that's a plug).

We've already examined ways of **expanding your candidate reach** but as a reminder – employee referral programs, easier application processes, going mobile – there are a number of ways to attract more candidates into your pipeline.

Research and prepare for the interview to the same degree that you would expect your candidate to. Even if you have an HR department they won't necessarily know all of the answers, especially when it comes to technical roles. And if you aren't an expert, YOU probably won't know the answers! If in doubt get advice on effective interview questions, even if it means consulting someone outside your company.

Review the social media profiles of your candidates on *LinkedIn*, *Twitter* and *Facebook* – in fact wherever they have an online profile. The way in which they directly engage with friends, colleagues and followers online – especially on 'SOCIAL' accounts will provide intriguing (or possibly otherwise!) insights into their personality.

Keep your brand message consistent across all of your market channels. I've already said this but you need to always be looking and thinking about your future superstars, not just the talent you need today.

The Millennials are coming and you had better be ready. By 2025, 75% of the global workforce is expected to consist of Generation Y with their 'big demands and high expectations', as described by Deloitte's 2014 Millennial Survey. I've provided a few tips on integrating them into your workforce in Appendix Two.

Appendix Two

6 Tips For Millennial Management

Generation Y – the Millennials who are joining your workforce now - are typically professionals born between 1980 and 2000. Unlike many of us who may fall into Generation X or the Baby Boomer generation, Millennials have a completely different set of characteristics and habits. These have evolved from their child-centric, often structured lives, and regular contact with a diverse range of people.

Millennials generally work well in teams, enjoy making friends in the working environment, have a 'can-do' attitude and seek out variety in their tasks. They also need regular feedback but are confident of fulfilling every task you set them. Generation Y is ready to take on the world!

They seek leadership, structure and a challenge but they cannot tolerate boredom. They are THE most connected generation in history, having grown up in a world of social media, text messages and email.

Yet again, I could write a book on Millennials in the workplace but my recommendation is that you download your own copy of Deloitte's Millennial Survey for 2014. That provides you with the essential information you need to know on the subject.

In the meantime, how do you as a business owner integrate Generation Y with the old school Generation X and even older school, soon to be retiring, Baby Boomers?

A panel held in New York in 2013, hosted by executives from international brands such as Johnson and Johnson and Ernst and

Young (EY), formulated six essential ways in which companies can work with Millennials to enhance their brands.

There's no straightforward answer but I found this advice extremely helpful:

Create a flexible working environment

Gone is the 'one size fits all' working environment. While flexibility is not the exclusive demand of Millennials, their influence is forcing companies to look at issues such as work/life balance in more detail. All generations value flexibility, closely followed by cash and benefits. The traditional work model of 9 to 5 is evolving.

Learn from your Millennials!

In a case of 'reverse mentoring', you might be surprised at what THEY can teach YOU! Parents of teenagers will know that they can teach us quite a lot in areas such as technology and social media - and EY backs this up, going so far as to suggest they can also provide assistance on issues in the workplace such as collaborating online. It makes sense to me.

Provide formal training opportunities

Millennials are more likely to be qualified to degree level but still require formal on-the-job training for hard AND soft skills. They crave career advice – it's up to you as the employer to provide it.

Provide subtle mentoring

Panel suggestions included: managers encouraging Millennials through twelve five-minute breaks for quick chats, rather than one solid hour of a meeting or lunch, for example. More frequent mentoring helps to increase the Millennials' sense of value and in turn their loyalty to the employer.

Give them a purpose, rather than perks

It's not about weekly massages and a 'nap' room in the office (I am not joking, it does happen!) Millennials are seeking a sense of purpose and the opportunity to grow in their role. In this case, it's traditional rather than trendy employee management that works.

Don't get caught up in stereotypes

Forget the Millennials' stereotypical qualities of entitlement and laziness. All generations think the ones that follow 'never had it so good'. Ultimately, everyone works to make money in a way that gives life meaning. Keep communication channels – and your mind – open to integrate Millennials into the workforce for a win-win scenario.

Appendix Three

Forty Non-Competency-Based Interview Questions For Employers

What Are Non-Competency-Based Questions?

Non-competency-based questions cover general topics and will provide the interviewer with an overview of the candidate's career history and reasons for leaving their current position.

Generally, employers use them to make the candidates feel more comfortable before asking the more probing competency-based questions.

I've included my choice of the most common non-competency-based questions below:

Question 1: Tell me about yourself

Question 2: Why do you want to work here/leave your current job?

Question 3: What makes you the best candidate for this job?

Question 5: What are your weaknesses?

Question 6: Where do you see yourself in five years' time?

Question 7: What do you think is your greatest achievement?

Question 8: Have you ever accepted a job you regretted taking?

Question 9: Imagine you are fresh out of school. Would you choose a different career path to the one you are on?

Question 10: Why is there a gap in your career history?

Question 11: What does success look like for you?

Question 12: Let's turn that around. What does failure look like for you?

Question 13: Why do you want to leave your current job?

Question 14: How do you handle criticism of your work?

Question 15: Would your colleagues say you thrive under pressure?

Question 16: Do you enjoy working in a team environment or do you prefer working alone?

Question 17: How would you resolve this problem?

Question 18: What made you choose this particular career path?

Question 19: How will you achieve your career goals?

Question 20: Can you work without supervision?

Question 21: What do you know about this company?

Question 22: What is it that this company can offer you?

Question 23: Describe your ideal job

Question 24: What is your experience of management?

Question 25: What efforts have you made to develop your skills and/or knowledge base?

Question 26: Are you willing to travel or relocate for the right role?

Question 27: Who has been a role model for you during your career?

Question 28: How would you deal with a colleague reporting to you who was clearly underperforming?

Question 29: How do you handle conflict?

Question 30: Would your colleagues say you are a good team player?

Question 31: What is the most difficult situation you have faced during your career

Question 32: Do you have any difficult colleagues that you struggle to work with?

Question 33: How do you influence and motivate your team?

Question 34: Do you respond well to being mentored?

Question 35: What's the riskiest thing you have done during your career?

Question 36: Give me an example of when you took the initiative in your current role?

Question 37: Do you lose your temper easily?

Question 38: Would your colleagues say you are trustworthy?

Question 39: What character traits make you perfect for this role?

Question 40: Describe yourself in three words.

APPENDIX FOUR

COMPETENCY-BASED INTERVIEW QUESTIONS

Competency-based interview questions are designed to test a specific skill, and you should note down the answers so you can compare one interviewee answer against the others.

Key Competencies that you should be 'testing' and questions that will help you dig beneath the service are:

Adaptability

Tell me about a time you've had to make a big change and how you coped with it?

Communication

Verbal Skills – Give me an example of a time where you had to explain something complex to a colleague, and how you overcame any problems this represented?

Listening Skills – Can you describe a time when you had to deal with an angry customer/colleague?

Written Skills - Do you prefer to write a report or prepare an oral presentation? Why?

Decision-Making Ability

What was the last big decision you had to make, and how did you arrive at that decision?

Explain a time where you have had to make a decision on your own without running it past your line manager first? How did it work out?

Innovation & Creativity

Tell me about a time where you had a new idea or a new way of doing something?

Influencing/Sales

Tell me about your best sales experience?

Tell me about your worst selling experience?

When have you successfully overcome a customer objection?

When have you failed to sell an idea or proposition that you really believed in? How did it make you feel?

Integrity

Can you explain a time when someone has asked you to do something that you objected to? How did you handle this situation?

What would you do if you were asked by your boss to do something illegal?

Independence

Can you recall a time where you had to go against established thinking in order to meet an objective?

Leadership

Have you ever faced reluctance from your team to move in the direction you wanted? How did you deal with this?

Have you ever had to adapt your leadership style to get the desired results? How?

Tell me about an instance where you were less successful as a leader than you would have wanted?

Risk Taking

What is the biggest risk you have taken and how did you handle this process?

Teamwork

What was the highest (or lowest) performing team you have ever worked in? What made it so?

How do you go about building relationships in the teams you work within?

Printed in Great Britain
by Amazon.co.uk, Ltd.,
Marston Gate.